PROTECT YOUR PERSONAL INFORMATION

Anzar Hasan & Abbas Mirza

Order this book online at www.trafford.com
or email orders@trafford.com

Most Trafford titles are also available at major online book retailers.

Print information available on the last page.

ISBN: 978-1-4907-7525-8 (sc)
ISBN: 978-1-4907-7527-2 (hc)
ISBN: 978-1-4907-7526-5 (e)

Library of Congress Control Number: 2016911463

Trafford rev.   09/16/2016

 www.trafford.com

North America & international
toll-free: 1 888 232 4444 (USA & Canada)
fax: 812 355 4082

This book is dedicated to our wonderful parents who taught us, try not to become a man of success, but rather try to become a man of value.

Contents

Preface

This is a book that is going to provide you with detailed information about the threats that you and your computer face when you enter the world of the Internet. It will discuss different ways through which you can protect yourself from intruders. This book covers all the major kinds of threats that you face when you go online. The book will even discuss the threats that your kids face when they go online. Since kids are not experienced and they are unaware of the consequences of the step they are going to take, thus it is important for the parents to know the dangers their kids face in the world of the Internet. It is the kind of book that you should read once you get to an age where you start using a computer and the Internet.

The book doesn't only highlight the issues that people face when they go online, but it also provides the solution to the problems. Not only this, but after reading the book, you will be able to get to know about different technical terms, the reason they present a threat to your computer, and the signals that you need to look for if you doubt you have become a victim. The book begins with the introduction to computer security and provides the reader with an overview of the issues and the threats that your computer could face if you do not care about it. The readers will be amazed to find the section on social media threats. Most people are not actually aware of the threats they face when they sign up on a social media website. Thus, this book is going to talk about ways to protect your identity even if you have signed up for a social media website.

Anzar Hassan and Abbas Mirza are the writers of this book. They intend to take ahead the initiative of cybersecurity. They both developed G7 Security in the year 2010 while working under Arshnet Technologies. This app can currently be found on the App Store. It was one of the most operative steps that were taken in order to educate people about cybersecurity. It was extremely important to launch it because people were not able to find a viable solution to the problem of cyber attacks. G7 Security is a cybersecurity research and global information security services entity. This entity offers research and development, information sharing, and collaboration. In addition to this, it offers various services for the information and cybersecurity community. The efforts made to develop the G7 Security app were recognized in Computerworld's Mobile Access awards category for the innovative application of IT. The major aim of this app was to extend the distribution of digital information, programs, and services through mobile devices. This was the reason due to which it was able to reach to the areas where use of mobile devices is quite common. The Computerworld Honors Program honors those who try to develop visionary applications of information technology through which they try to promote positive social, economic, and educational change.

The authors' basic aim behind this book is to ensure that a nontechnical person gets to know about the threats and dangers that he and his devices face once he connects himself to the Internet. This book plays an important role in fulfilling the basic aim of the authors. After reading this book, you will be able to realize the fact that you were living life in danger by connecting your computer to the Internet. But by following the right steps, you will be able to secure your device and your identity from being misused.

Chapter 1

AN INTRODUCTION TO COMPUTER SECURITY

Protect Your Computer from Being Vulnerable to Attacks
Accessing the Internet on your computer is pretty common these days. The Internet will provide you the ease of accessing numerous products and services while sitting back home. With such ease comes the danger of attacks of viruses and other damaging elements. Use of the Internet exposes your computer to scammers, hackers, and identity thieves.

Computer Security
When you access the Internet, there are several scammers, hackers, and identity thieves that are in search of a person whose personal information could be stolen and used for illegal purposes. Your money is also prone to these attacks. These dangers nullify the benefit of the Internet; thus there are steps introduced to protect your computer from these dangerous elements. Some of the common preventions that you have heard from elders are not to provide your personal information without a valid reason and to keep your software up-to-date.

Use Security Software That Updates Automatically
There are too many bad guys who are always trying to find a way to attack your computer. They are always making an effort

to find a new way to attack your computer and to access your personal information. Thus, it is highly important that you keep your software updates so that it helps protect you against the threats. There are numerous security software that can update all by themselves. You should try to use this kind of software on your computer so that, even if you forget to update, your computer is secure from attacks. There are several such companies who offer free security software from well-known companies. You should alter your operating system and web browser settings so that they update regularly. If you are not going to make sure that your software is up-to-date, then you are providing them a way to attack your computer. You should avoid buying security software from the companies that claim that they have found malware on your computers because they are actually the scammers who send in messages to get access to your computer.

Your Personal Information Is Just like Cash
Your personal information is extremely important and you need to value it as you value your cash. Scammers will try their best to present themselves as trustworthy, but you need to be careful about the fact that this information is highly confidential.

Research About the Companies You Are Really Dealing With
Research can save you from scams and other dangerous acts that you might get involved in just because your personal information was leaked on the Internet. Usually people go after the ad or the offer that looks quite attractive and then get scammed. So if you find any kind of ad or offer on the Internet just spare time to research about the company. Just type the company name with the words *reviews, complaint,* or *scam* on Google or any other search engine you prefer to use. If you find negative reviews then understand one thing—that you are on the wrong side. If you are not able to find anything then again understand that there are some issues with that.

Ensure That You Give out Your Personal Information over Encrypted Websites Only

When you are shopping online or making a banking transaction, then you need to ensure that the website uses encryption to protect your information. When the information travels from the computer to the server, then it is vulnerable to the attacks. To make sure that the website is encrypted, ensure that the website address is written as *https*. The *s* at the end states that the website is secure.

There are a few websites that use encryption only on the sign-in page. Thus, you need to make sure that each page contains security. If each page doesn't have the required security, then the website is surely vulnerable to attack, and you are risking your information.

Safeguard Your Passwords

It is recommended that you should use strong passwords so that it is difficult for others to crack and use your information for illegal means. The following are some of the guidelines that will help you keep strong passwords:

- It is advised that you should use long passwords because it is difficult to crack long passwords. The ideal length of a strong password is ten to twelve characters.
- Try to mix letters, special characters, and numbers so that your password becomes challenging to crack. Just make sure that your password is unpredictable. There is no need to use your name, birth date, or common words as these things make your password predictable.
- Although passwords are difficult to remember, it is still advisable to use different passwords for different accounts. In case one of the accounts is hacked and the password is stolen, then there is a fair chance that your other accounts have become vulnerable to attacks as well.
- Sharing passwords on the phone through texts and e-mails is quite dangerous. Legitimate companies will make sure

that they do not ask for your password through messages. If you do get such a message, then it is surely a scam.

- You need to make sure that all the passwords are kept in a secure place.

Make Sure You Back Up Your Files
It is a fact that the systems made by humans are not 100 percent secure. It is extremely important to copy the important files on a removable disc or in an external hard drive, and keep it in a safe place. This will ensure that your data is completely safe even if your computer is compromised.

Securing Your Wireless Network
In this modern age, the wireless home network has numerous devices connected to them like our computers, phones, cameras, and even our televisions as well. It is extremely important to take steps to secure our wireless networks as these will ultimately help to secure your devices and your information from being compromised.

Try to Understand the Way a Wireless Network Works
When you go wireless you actually connect to Internet access points. A wireless router sends signals through the air. If you have a strong router then it may send signals as far as a hundred feet. If you have a wireless network, then any device within the range can pull the signal from the air and it can easily access the Internet.

If you do not take precautions, then anyone coming within the range of your router can access your network. If you have any hacker in your neighborhood they could "piggyback" on your network, or he could easily access your information on your device. If your network is used to commit a crime or send spam, then you are going to be held accountable for it even if you do not even know about it.

Use of Encryption Is the Best Way to Secure Your Network

It is extremely important to encrypt your data while sending it over the network. This is extremely important so that the attackers nearby are not able to eavesdrop on these communications. Encryption is actually a process in which the information is scrambled into some kind of code so that if anyone gets access to that information he is not able to decode it. It is one of the most effective ways to secure the data sent over the network.

There are two main types of encryptions available for this particular purpose. The first one is known as Wi-Fi Protected Access (WPA) and the other is known as Wired Equivalent Privacy (WEP). Your computer, router, and other equipment use the same encryption. Wi-Fi Protected Access II (WPA2) is one of the strongest encryptions available and if you are given an option for that, then try and opt for it. This particular type of encryption is going to protect your information from these hackers. Usually older routers use only WEP encryption thus the devices connected to that particular device is vulnerable to common hacking problems. If you have a router that uses WEP then you need to buy a new router immediately that has a WAP2 capability.

When you buy the router you will find the encryption feature turned off so the first thing you need to do is to turn this feature on. You will be provided with the instructions in a manual that is going to help you with the way to turn the encryption option on. You can also check the router company's website to check out the steps if you are not given a manual along with the router.

Bound Access to Your Network

Since there are just a few devices in your house that can access your home network thus you need to allow only these devices to access the network. You should make sure that you limit the access of extra devices that access your network. Each device comes with a media access control (MAC) address that uniquely identifies each and every device. Wireless routers come with an ability to allow only those devices whose MAC addresses are permitted to use the network. But some of the hackers have impersonated MAC addresses as well thus you should not only rely on this step alone.

Make Sure Your Router Is Secure

It is extremely important to keep your router secure from different attacks. Your router is responsible for directing the traffic between your local network and the Internet. If you do not take proper steps to secure your router then someone may take control over it and could gain access to your personal information, or he might seize the control of your router and may direct you toward fraudulent websites. The following are some of the common steps that are going to allow you to secure your router from different attacks:

- Change your router name.
  When you buy the router it comes along with a default name. You have the liberty to change the name of the router. The name of the router is commonly known as service set identifier, or SSID. You need to make sure you change the name to a unique one.

- Change the default password on your router.
  Since the networks are vulnerable to attacks the router manufacturing companies add a default password for the router. Hackers are pretty much aware of the default passwords thus it is recommended to change these passwords to unique ones. You need to follow the tips for the having strong passwords so that your router is secure from attacks.

- Do not use "Remote Management" features.
  Some routers offer the feature of remote access, but this option makes your router vulnerable to attacks. Thus, it is recommended to turn this option off as hackers could easily get into your home network through this particular option.

- Make sure you log out as Administrator.
  When you log in, your session is stored and it is not destroyed until or unless you log out. If you leave your admin account logged in, then hackers can use the details from your session to gain access to your router.

- Update your router regularly.
  When you buy a router, software comes along with them. You need to make sure that the software that comes along with the router is updated regularly. You just have to check the option that says that you want to occasionally update the software. Before installing the router, just make sure if there is a new version available on the manufacturer's site. You can even register on the manufacturer's website so that you receive the information about the latest updates.

- Make sure you secure your computer along with your router.
  You must be aware of the basic rules available to secure your computer. Just follow them so that your computer is secure as well. You need to make sure that the antivirus is up-to-date and the firewall settings are good enough to ensure that your computer is safe from attacks.

Protect Your Network during Mobile Access
Since the introduction of smartphones, the applications on the phone allow you to access your home network through a mobile device. Before you connect your phone, you need to make sure that you have taken care of the security features. You should use a strong password on the app that accesses your home network. You need to make sure that you log out of the app after using it so that the session is destroyed and no one is able to access your account if your phone is stolen. You need to protect your phone with a password. This feature is going to enhance the security of your phone.

Chapter 2

HOW TO ENSURE SECURITY OF COMPUTER

Home Network Security
In this section, the users will get an overview of the security risks and the countermeasures associated with Internet connectivity. The following details are especially important in the context of always-on broadband services. The following details mentioned are also relevant to the traditional dial-up users.

A. What is computer security?
Computer security is quite a self-explanatory term. It is a process which helps to prevent and detect unauthorized use of your computer. Prevention measures are going to help prevent unauthorized users from breaking into your computer while detection is going to assist you in detecting if any intruder breaks into your computer.

B. Why should I care about computer security?
Computers have become an essential part of our daily life. We use them for banking, investing, shopping, and communicating with others through e-mail or chat programs. You definitely do not consider your chats secret but your e-mails and banking transaction will be definitely be important for you. Thus, you will not want

anyone to access your personal information or attack other computers through your computer.

C. Who would want to break into my computer at home?
Hackers, attackers, or crackers will break into your computer. They might not care about your identity. Usually they get control of your computer so that they could attack your computer and launch attacks on other computers. This way the hackers can launch attacks from your computer and hide their own location so that they cannot be caught. When they are going to attack the high profile sites like government websites or the financial system then you will be caught as they are going to launch an attack from your computer. Even if you are connected to the Internet just to send e-mails or to play games, your computer might still be vulnerable to the attacks.

Intruders may be able to watch all your actions and they might even cause damage to your computer by reformatting your hard drive or changing your data.

D. How easy is it to break into my computer?
Intruders are always seeking a chance to attack the computer available online. These vulnerabilities are also known as "holes." These holes are present in the computer software. If the software is too complex then it becomes extremely difficult to check the security of the software.

When the holes are discovered, computer vendors will develop patches to address the problem. But it is left up to the user if they want to install those patches or not. Configuration of the software is also dependent upon the user as this way the software could operate more securely. There are several such incidents that report that the admin and the users could have been protected if they kept the system and the security software up-to-date.

Some of the applications have default settings that allow the users to access your computer. You should change the settings so that your computer is more secure. For instance, chat programs allow outsiders to execute commands on your computer or web browser so that a harmful program could be placed on your computer that will activate when you are going to click on it.

Good Security Habits

How Can You Minimize the Access Other People Have to Your Information?

If someone physically accesses your things, with your permission or without it, then it might be much easier to identify them as compared to those who remotely access your computer. As long as you may connect to the network your device is vulnerable to attacks of these kinds of remote hackers. But you can definitely secure your computer from these attacks. If you want to do it then you need to follow certain rules and regulations that are written as follows:

- Make sure that you lock your computer when you are away from it. You should make it your habit to lock it up even if you step away for a few moments. Locking would prevent others from accessing your personal information.
- You need to disconnect the computer from the Internet during the time when you are not using it. The technologies like DSL and cable modems have made it possible for users to be online all the time. But the convenience of being online all the time brings certain risks along with it. The chances of your computer being attacked by the hacker increase when you connect to the network 24/7. Disconnecting will mean that you turn off your Wi-Fi, disconnecting the cable from DSL, or turning off your computer.
- You need to evaluate your security settings and make sure that the settings do not make your computer vulnerable to

viruses. Enabling certain features may increase your risk of getting infected. Thus, it is important to check the settings when you install the software and change them according to your needs. If you hear about something that could affect your settings then evaluate the settings and ensure the safety of your laptop.

What Other Steps Can You Take?

Your data is not only vulnerable to attacks and viruses but it is also vulnerable to the natural or technological causes. Although you have no control over these aspects, you could at least prepare for this situation to minimize the loss.

- The first and foremost thing that you could do are to protect your computer against power outages. There are some surges that protect your computer from power surges. There are several such power surge companies out there who offer compensation if they do not protect your computer in the right way. Power strips are an effective solution to this problem because they do not only protect your computer from power outages but also offer an uninterruptable power supply in case of power surges or outages. When there is lightning or construction work going on, try keeping your laptop powered down because such situations often causes power surges.

- You need to back up all your data so that, in case you lose your computer, you do not lose the important data kept in your computer. You must have experienced losing files because of a virus or any other reason and you must have faced the circumstances of it as well. Thus, it is important that you regularly back up your computer on a CD or any other storage device so that the chances of losing data are minimized. Determining how often to back up your data is a personal decision. If you change your files rarely, then backing up once a month would be enough—while, if you make changes regularly, daily backups would prove useful.

Understanding AntiVirus Software

What Does Antivirus Software Do?

An antivirus is software that is responsible for keeping check on the files downloaded on the computer. It scans the files downloaded on the computer to check for certain patterns that may indicate whether there is malicious software present in the package downloaded or not. This particular software is also referred to as anti-malware software. The software looks for patterns that are based on the signatures or definitions that are called malware. The vendors of this software bring in updates frequently so that your files are secure from the newest and latest techniques that may harm your computer.

You have to install antivirus software once and scan your computer periodically to ensure that it is safe from malware.

1. *Automatic scans.* Almost all antivirus software come with an option to scan the computer automatically. For automatic scans, you have to set intervals, after which regular scans will be held.
2. *Manual scans.* The antivirus software may not have the option to scan your computer automatically after defining the scan, but it would definitely be able to scan the computer manually whenever you ask.
   - The attachments can bring in malware along with them. Thus, it is recommended to scan the attachments as they are downloaded.
   - The CDs and the DVDs also bring in malware along with them. Thus, you should scan them before opening the files.

How Will the Software Respond When It Finds Malware?

In most of the antivirus software, you will find a pop-up that is going to alert you that it has found malware on your computer. It will ask your permission on whether to clean the malware or not.

Some of the antivirus software is set in a way that they remove the virus without even informing the user. Before selecting the antivirus software, you need to read the description to ensure that they fulfill your requirements.

Which Software Should You Use?

There are numerous vendors that produce antivirus software—thus it is a difficult task to identify which one is the best for you. All antivirus software is basically the same, so your decisions will majorly be based upon the recommendations, features, availability, or the price. It doesn't matter what type of software you use; installing it would definitely increase the level of protection.

How Do You Get the Current Malware Information?

This particular process varies from product to product, so you need to figure out what your antivirus requires. There are several antivirus programs on the market that allow the user to automatically receive updated malware definitions. Since new information is added, it is an extremely good idea to take advantage of this particular option. If you receive e-mails related to your malware, then try confirming it from your vendor or the legal sources provided by the vendor. This is because these e-mails are usually hoaxes, and they can damage your computer. Antivirus software provide you with the easiest and most effective way to protect your computer. As the antivirus relies on the signatures, it can only recognize the software that has some known properties. Thus, it is recommended to keep the signatures up-to-date.

Using Caution with E-mail Attachments

Why Can E-mail Attachments Be Dangerous?

The following are some of the most common reason that make e-mail attachments opportune and prevalent. Moreover, they also become one of the most common tools for attackers.

- E-mails are easy to circulate. Forwarding an e-mail is a simple task as you can forward the e-mail to several recipients with a single click. Sending malware through e-mails infect the computer easily. There exist such viruses that do not even need users to forward the e-mail as they can scan the user addresses and forward the e-mail to all the contacts in the list.
- E-mail programs attempt to address almost all users' needs thus they allow the sender to attach any kind of file they want.
- E-mail programs try to be user friendly thus they automatically download the attachments which exposes your computer to viruses within the attachments.

What Steps Can You Take to Protect Yourself and Others in Your Address Book?

- Beware of the attachments that come through e-mails. These e-mails might look like they come from the vendors of the antivirus software, but actually these are the e-mails that contain malware and they might damage your computer.

- Ensure that the antivirus software is up-to-date. You need to ensure that you have installed the necessary updates so that your computer is safe from the latest malware. You should also enable the option of automatic updates. This will make your system safe from all the vulnerabilities of viruses.

- Trust your instincts to judge if the e-mail is malware or not. If you think that the e-mail is suspicious, then do not open it even if your antivirus gives a clear hit. The reason behind this is that the hackers are busy finding new ways to attack your computer. What you can do is contact the person who sent you the e-mail to make sure it is a legitimate e-mail. But if your instincts tell you that this is some kind of suspicious e-mail, then you must trust it and avoid opening such an e-mail.

- First, you need to save the attachment and then scan any of the attachment before opening them. If you want to open the attachment, then you need to verify the source by taking the following steps:
    1. Update your antivirus to the latest version.
    2. Save the file on your hard drive.
    3. Scan the file manually to check for viruses.
    4. If the file is clean, then go ahead.

- Do not allow your computer to download the attachments automatically. This feature is usually turned on to assist users in reading e-mail. If you have turned it on, then make sure to turn it off.

- Make separate accounts for all the users on your computer. Operating systems allow you the opportunity to create multiple accounts with different rights. You should also consider viewing e-mails with restricted privileges. This is because usually a virus needs admin rights to infect the computer.

- Apply additional security practices to your computer so that you are able to filter out particular types of attachments through e-mail software or firewall.

Password Security, Protection, and Management
From the way we use the Internet, it is easy to consider the fact that some passwords are a bit less important than the others. For us, all passwords should be important because we have our personal information stored on it and the wrongdoers can access that information to use it for their own benefit. They can even use the information to share on social media networks. Some of the

commercial websites allow customers to store the billing and the shipping information with the credit card information.

In this section of the book, you will learn the recommendations for protecting your information by choosing strong passwords and managing these passwords safely. In this part of the book, you will also find some of the common mistakes and the remedies for managing passwords.

Every Password Is Important

From the way we use the Internet, it is easy to consider the fact that some passwords are a bit less important than the others. For us, all passwords should be important because we have our personal information stored on it and the wrongdoers can access that information to use it for their own benefit. They can even use the information to share on social media networks. Some of the commercial websites allow customers to store the billing and the shipping information with the credit card information.

Creating and Protecting Your Passwords

Wrongdoers previously used complex methods to gain access to your personal information, but now these methods are becoming a whole lot easier and much more effective than they were before. Thus, it is extremely important to avoid the mistakes that most of the individuals make to exploit your private information.

Common Mistakes and Remedies

Mistake 1

The first and foremost mistake that people make is that they use weak passwords for their personal accounts. Some of the common examples of weak passwords would be a common phrase such as your name, birth date, *password*, or anything that could be guessed easily.

Remedy 1

The easiest way to create a password is to use a passphrase. Microsoft Safety and Security Center demonstrates a good example, which is stated below.

- Start with a sentence or two as complex passwords are hard to guess
- You need to remove the spaces between the words.
- For instance, "Complexpasswordsaresafer" could be a good password because it is a misspelled word.
- To make these passwords more complex you can add a number at the end of the phrase such as "ComplekspasswordsRsafer2011"

The above-mentioned activity shows the proper way to use complex and strong password for your accounts. The above-mentioned passwords use several safe password guidelines such as it is long, it is not a common phrase, and it includes numbers and both uppercase and lowercase letters. You could even include a special sign to make it more complex.

Mistake 2

Since remembering passwords is not an easy task people usually use one password for all the accounts they have. This is a major security concern because hackers might get access to all your accounts having the same password. If the hacker gets access to the password for a non-sensitive account, then he can use the information on sites for other purposes such as billing, payment, and health.

It is recommended that you use different passwords for each account and even the pattern of password should not be the same because hackers are smart and they can crack into your sensitive accounts as well.

Remedy 2

You should try to use a different password for each website you enter. If you forget the passwords, then you could use password managers. Password managers are an encrypted database that could help you to store all the unique passwords in one safe place.

Mistake 3

You should make sure that you do not log in to your sensitive account in public or even in front of a person whom you trust. You should not keep a note of your password to yourself or share your password with others in any way. If your browser offers you to remember a password, then just reject the offer. This is because browsers usually do not encode in a safe way. Password recovery tools enable anyone to see all the passwords stored in the browser and open user profiles.

Remedy 3

The basic thing you could do is to avoid using public computers and accessing unsecured networks. If you have no other options then avoid accessing the private information, or change the password as soon as possible. You also need to avoid sharing passwords with people. You might have a guest who requests to access your home network so, instead of telling him the password, type it yourself.

Password Managers

Password managers are there to ease out the problem of those people who have an issue with forgetting their passwords. A password manager is going to keep all your passwords in one place and it will be accessible through one master phrase. It is one of the best ways to keep a record of all the passwords you use. When you use password managers you will have to remember only one master phrase to access all the passwords thus you will be free from the hassle of remembering various passwords.

Types of Password Managers

There are several different types of password managers available in the market. A desktop password manager is the most common of all. This is software that is installed on your computer's hard drive.

The other type of password manager is a portable one that will allow you to use the password manager anywhere and anytime. These password managers are usually on the smartphone and other portable devices. Or you can even choose to store passwords online in a password management provider's website or choose multi-factor authentication. For instance, you could use a fingerprint to access the contents or any other source of authentication could also prove useful as well.

This would help to reduce the efforts you apply to learn numerous different passwords.

Since the technological advancements have reached their peak, there is a much more secure way introduced to save your passwords. They are trying to use cloud technology to provide you with password managers. Your passwords will be securely stored in the cloud while each of your devices will have a synchronized local copy of the passwords saved, irrespective of the software platform that you are using. Cloud providers are also going to back up your file regularly so that you do not lose content.

Choosing the Right Password Manager

While choosing, remember the circumstances for where it will be used. While choosing the password manager, you need to ensure the circumstances for where it will be used. For instance, if you will be storing only the passwords of the sites that you will only access at home, then there is no need to store the password manager on the mobile device. Considering another situation in which one wants to access the password manager on the go, then he might need to have an app that will stay in his phone along with him. Numerous websites have now started allowing one-time passwords for all your accounts so that you need not have a number of passwords to remember. But you need to be careful to remember the time period that particular password is valid for.

First of all, you need to make sure that acquiring a password manager is the best solution to manage your passwords and usernames.

When you are aware of your need, then you can investigate that particular product. Before choosing a password manager just be sure of the following points:

- Does the password manager use strong encryption?
- Does it have a lockout feature?
- Does it include protection from malicious activity?

Evaluate Ease of Use and Convenience
You need to evaluate the password manager to make sure of where it stands. Review the functionality and the features of the software.

Consider Cost
Is it worth buying the software? Is it a one-time cost or do you have to pay regularly after small periods of time? If you have to pay for the software, does it have features worth paying for?

First, add your own reviews on it and then go online to get reviews of the product.

Finally, Keep the Risks in Mind
Keeping your passwords on the cloud will give you the edge of being portable but, along with that, it will come with the risk of potential attacks on cloud password managers. In May 2011, Brennan Slattery reported in a PC World article that there was some unusual activity going on thus all the customers were advised to change their master password.

You also need to remember that there is a huge risk if you access password managers in public locations. It is a big risk if you leave your password manager open in the background. If you leave the password manager on a public computer, then you are taking a big risk as it may contain all your passwords. On public computers, keylogging software is being used on the computers. This software will capture the information that you type, and the malicious user could get your password, and he could crack into your accounts.

The best way to protect your master password is to memorize it because writing it down is not a viable or a secure solution.

Some Concluding Words on Password Managers

Passwords are one necessary element of the modern world. They help keep our information secure from being accessed by wrongdoers. Password managers have presented us with a useful solution to the problem of managing all kinds of passwords. They are one of the most beneficial and expedient inventions of the modern age where protecting personal information has become such a big issue. There are several guidelines that are going to help us keep secure passwords. These guidelines are also going to help us choose the right password manager for you.

Before you make the final decision on a password manager, you first have to use it for a trial period. Then you will have to read reviews online about its performance and the shortcomings so that you can know that you are spending bucks on software that is worth it. After choosing the right password manager for yourself, you need to make sure you buy the software directly from the vendor. While installing the software, make sure that the person is not installing the modified version of the software. You can check this by checking an MD5 hash of the installer. If the hash is not available, ask the vendor to provide it himself. If the vendor is not able to provide the verification method, then be skeptical. Although it will take some effort to move to a password manager, in the long run, it will prove to be one useful and secure way to protect your passwords and guard your personal information.

The Dos and Don'ts

A laptop brings in the factor of portability—but along with that, it brings in a lot of danger to your personal information. A minor irresponsibility could lead to a lost laptop. If it goes missing, then all the valuable information stored on it may get into the hands of hackers and identity thieves. The following are some of the dos and don'ts that could help you protect your laptop from being stolen:

Do:
- Your laptop is as important as your cash. Treat it like you treat your cash.
- Ensure physical security by locking it with a cable.
- Remain alert in public places like airports and hotels.
- Try to make your laptop smart by adding an alarm to it.
- Try to carry your laptop in a case that is a bit less obvious. Carry a handbag that can fit your laptop in easily.

Don't:
- Do not leave your laptop unattended.
- Avoid putting your laptop on the floor.
- Do not leave your laptop in your car unattended.
- Avoid keeping passwords in laptop cases.

The Dos

Treat your laptop just you treat you like cash.
How would you treat your cash in a public place? Would you let everyone know that you have a huge sum of money in your pocket? Will you show off cash to the public? Obviously not. Similarly, you should treat your laptop in the same way. It is important to keep the same watchful eye on your laptop as you would on your cash.

Ensure physical security by locking it with a cable.
When you are in a public place just tie your laptop with a security cable. Attach that cable with something that is not easy to remove or that is quite heavy.

Remain alert in public places like airports and hotels.
When you go through the security at airports there is a fair chance that you might lose sight of your laptop thus it is extremely important to keep an eye on your laptop as you go through the security check. You should hold on to it tightly until the person in front of you has gone through the metal detector. You should also keep an eye on it when it emerges out on the other side. The confusion and the shuffling that occur in security checkpoints can become solid grounds for theft.

If you are on a visit, then a security cable will definitely not be enough to secure your laptop. Thus, you need to ensure that you secure your laptop in a safe place in your room.

Try to make your laptop smart by adding an alarm to it.
Needs vary from person to person; thus an alarm could be a useful addition to your laptop. Some laptops have an alarm sound when there is unexpected motion or when the computers are away from a specified range. You can even install a program that lets you know about the location of your computer once it is connected to the Internet.

Try to carry your laptop in a case that is a bit less obvious. Carry such a handbag that can fit in your laptop easily.
When you are on the road, carrying the laptop in a laptop case might announce it to the world that you are carrying a laptop inside. You should use a suitcase or a backpack so that it is not prominent to the world that you are carrying something like a laptop.

The Don'ts

Do not leave your laptop unattended.
You might trust your college fellows a lot, but it is still not advisable to leave your computer unattended. Although the people may seem nice and helpful, they are not the ones who will be forced to buy

a new laptop; so make sure you take along the laptop wherever you go. Or if it's not possible to take it along, then tie it up with something heavy so that it's difficult for someone to steal it.

Avoid putting your laptop on the floor.
It doesn't matter if you are in public or not; just make sure that you do not put your laptop on floor. If there is no other option, then the best way is to put it between your legs so that you remember that you have a belonging that you have to carry.

Do not leave your laptop in your car unattended.
Parked cars are an easy target for thieves. If you have no other option than leaving your laptop in the car, then make sure that you hide it under the seat or somewhere it is not easily visible.

Avoid keeping passwords in laptop cases.
As mentioned above, you need to have strong passwords in order to ensure the security of your computer, but the problem that comes along with strong passwords is that they are difficult to remember. Thus, a lot of people leave the passwords in their cases, which is extremely dangerous. This way, it will become a whole lot easier for the thief to get to your personal information.

Where to Report a Stolen Laptop
In case your laptop is stolen, the first thing that you need to do is to report to the authorities.

- If it is your personal laptop, then your identity is at risk; thus you need to visit fits. Gov/idtheft.
- If the laptop is provided by the company that you work in, then immediately inform the employer. You must review the FTC's information related to the breaches.

Holiday Traveling with Personal Internet-Enabled Devices

Know the Risks
All the devices you possess are all computers such as your phone tablet or any other device. These devices are open to the chance of being attacked just like your computer. Thus, it is extremely important to take the same precautions with these things as you take precautions with your computer. Since these devices are portable they also need to be protected physically. In addition to that, you need to ensure that you do not use an unsecure Internet connection on these devices.

Do Not Use Public Wi-Fi Networks
Open Wi-Fi and the Wi-Fi you find in hotels, cafés, and other places are unsecure, and they present a huge risk for the information that you transmit through them. Thus, you should avoid using these connections because your device may be prone to attack due to the insecurity of the connection. You should try using cellular data instead of Wi-Fi in order to make any financial transaction or transmitting any sensitive information.

Turn Off Bluetooth When Not in Use
Bluetooth-enabled devices are prone to attack. The attackers will pair with your phone through Bluetooth, and they may steal your personal information. Thus, after using Bluetooth, you should switch it off so that your phone is not available for connection.

Be Cautious When Charging
Do not connect your phone to someone's computer for charging. You should also avoid using the charging stations available at the airport, library, café, or any other public place. When you connect with the computer, your phone software interacts with the software in the computer; and if the computer is compromised, then there is a fair chance that your phone will be compromised too.

What to Do If Your Accounts Are Compromised

You will definitely know once there is something wrong with your account. The first thing that you need to do when you know that your account is hacked is to call the bank or the credit card company. Notify them to block your card. Secondly, you should change all your passwords for the online services you use. You can visit http://www.idtheft.gov/ to see more information if you have suffered because of identity theft.

Debunking Some Common Myths

How are these myths established?

Myths are formed because people do not have complete information about a particular topic. There's no specific reason for myths. Most of the myths written below are based on assumptions, generalized knowledge of a specific area, or some other source. These myths are passed from one person to another as they seem legitimate enough to be true.

Why is it important to know the truth?

These myths might make you relax a lot in your security habits. You need to be diligent about the protection of your computer because otherwise you will be more likely to become a victim of an attack.

What are some common myths, and what is the truth behind them?

- Myth: Antivirus software and firewalls are 100 percent effective.

The truth is that an antivirus software and the firewall play a significant role in protecting your computer, but they do not guarantee 100 percent to protect your computer from attack. By combining these activities, you will be able to significantly reduce the risk of an attack.

- Myth: Once the software is installed on your computer, you do not have to worry about it anymore.

It is not true that once the software is installed on your computer, it will not require any updates. Vendors release updated versions frequently—thus it is important to update your software regularly in order to remove any kind of vulnerability.

- Myth: There is nothing important on your machine, so you do not need to protect it.

It is not about the information in your laptop as there are people who do not secure their laptop because they consider their computer invulnerable to attack because there is no important information kept in their laptop. But the reality is that your laptop might be used for launching attacks on other computers.

- Myth: Attackers only target people with money.

Usually, attackers look for people who have financial information stored in their computers. Attackers can make anyone a victim of identity theft. Attackers want maximum results out of an attack thus they target the databases that store financial information. Thus, it is extremely important to pay attention to credit card information so that you could minimize the chance of potential damage.

- Myth: When computers slow down, it means that they are old and should be replaced.

People usually replace computers when they feel that their computer is getting slow. If you are running heavy software on old computers, then it is possible that your computer might get slow. But if buying a new computer is not an option, you may upgrade your computer. Another possibility is that there may be programs running in the background. Your computer might be compromised by malware or spyware.

Chapter 3

INTRODUCTION TO MALWARE

Viruses and spyware are one of the most common issues in this modern age where communication has become so easy. There are certain steps that can help to protect your computer from viruses and spyware. When we state the word *malware* then we mean viruses, spyware, and other unwanted software that resides on your computer without your consent. These programs may cause your device to crash and they might use these programs to monitor and control your activity. Unwanted software is going to make your computer more vulnerable to the inappropriate ads that you do not want to see on your computer. Criminals use these malware to access your personal information or send spam or to commit different kinds of frauds.

Avoid Malware
Scam artists are always trying to find a way to trick people by persuading them to click the links that will download viruses, spyware, and other unwanted software on your computer. They usually bundle the malware with free downloads. Thus, you need to follow a few steps in order to protect your computer from these attacks.

- You should make sure that there is updated security software installed on your computer. In addition to this, there should be sufficient firewall settings to protect your computer from being at risk of attack. You also need to ensure that your operating system, antivirus, and browser are set to update automatically.

- There is no need to change your browser's security setting. You may minimize "drive-by" or bundled downloads if the settings of your browser are at default.

- You need to pay attention to your browser's warnings. Numerous browsers come with built-in security settings; thus they might warn you when downloading a file or before you visit an infected webpage.

- You should avoid clicking links that come in e-mails because they might be scammed. You need to ensure that you type the address of the company directly into the URL and access the website that way. Using e-mail to send scam is one of the ways used to catch prey.

- Avoid opening the attachments in the e-mails until or unless you are completely sure that this file is not a virus. Opening a wrong attachment, even from a trusted partner, may cause a malware to install on your computer.

- Do not get the software from a website that offers a lot of software. This means that they are more likely to include malware. Thus, it is recommended to get software directly from the official website.

- While installing the software, read each and every screen, and make sure that you are not installing bundled software along with it. If the software does come with it then decline the option of the additional software or exit the installation.

- There is no need to click on the ads that say that your computer's performance is low or we have detected a virus in your computer. This is because scammers have inserted unwanted software in the banner ads. Although the banners look legitimate they contain malware.

- Before using any external storage device you need to scan it for viruses. These devices get infected if you use them in high traffic places like public computers.

- Educate your family about safe computing. Let them know about the consequences of malware and other viruses. You need to tell them that downloading "free" games or programs, opening chain e-mails, or posting personal information is quite risky.
- Make sure that you back up your data regularly so that, in case you lose your computer due to malware, you will not lose the important files.

Detect Malware

You need to keep a check on your computer. If your computer is infected with malware then it may do the following:

- It slows down, crashes, or displays repeated error messages.
- You are not able to shut it down.
- You see a barrage of pop-ups.
- Your computer serves inappropriate ads or such ads that interfere with page content.
- It won't let you uninstall unwanted software.
- It injects ads in places which are ad-free like government websites.
- It starts to display unwanted web pages and sends e-mails that you do not intend to send.

Some other common problems that computers face when they are attacked by malware:

- You see new and unexpected toolbars in your browser or on your desktop.
- Your browser looks completely changed and your search engine has been changed from the default to some other one. Your browser may open tabs by itself.
- Your home page changes repeatedly.
- Laptop battery drains out quicker than expected.

Get Rid of Malware

If you have doubts that your computer has the above-mentioned elements, then you need to follow the following steps:

- Avoid doing activities that involve any kind of password. Try and ensure that you do not shop, make any banking transaction, or any such things that will endanger your personal information.
- Install and update security software and scan your computer for virus and spyware. Delete the files that cause problems. If the computer asks for a restart, then let it restart.
- Ensure that your browser has tools to delete the malware. If it doesn't have, then reset your browser to factory settings.
- If your computer is new and it offers technical support, then it is advisable to contact the manufacturer. Before your visit, just write down your model number and the serial number of your product. In addition to that write down the software that you installed, when your computer started to misbehave, and a short description of the problem.

There are several companies that offer technical support, but if you do not have the option of technical support, then try to contact an expert through a telephone. This might prove to be a cheap way to resolve the issue. Do not go for online search results because the solutions might be posted by the scammers to which you are facing the current problem. They do this to boost up their ranking in search engines so that their websites and phone numbers appear above those of legitimate companies. You may even contact the tech support of the software that you are using.

P2P File-Sharing Risks

P2P file sharing is commonly practiced in this modern age and it brings along a lot of risks that we are going to discuss in this chapter. P2P file sharing is basically a process in which files like music and games are shared over a peer to peer network. There is special software that connects the computers running the same software. It sometimes gives access to millions of computers at a time, but, at the same time, the risk of getting scammed also increases. The following are some of the common issues that a lot of people have faced due to this type of sharing:

- People usually download malware, pirated or copyrighted material, and/or pornography.
- This may allow strangers to access and share your personal files.

Now it must be clear to you why P2P sharing is not considered a reliable source of sharing content. But you may take a few steps to minimize these risks.

Try to Install Reputable Security Software

Some file-sharing programs may let malware get into your computer so that criminals could get access to your information and they could monitor and control your activity. Thus, you should use the following precautions before using any file-sharing program:

- First of all, you need to install a reputable security program. You need to make sure that the security program you are using should have antivirus and antispyware protection.
- You need to make sure that your security software and operating system is up-to-date.
- Immediately delete files that cause the problem.
- Make sure that you have made a backup of the files that are important.
- Before opening the downloaded file, just make sure that you have scanned it thoroughly.

If your P2P file asks you to change your firewall settings, then you must reconsider once before opening it. Changing the settings of your firewall may weaken your computer.

Bound Yourself From Sharing and Its Frequency

You must be aware of the folders that you are sharing. You need to install files and folders from P2P carefully and understand the fact that not all the folders are there to be made public. These programs are basically designed to share the files. But once these programs are installed on your computer, they may share the files and the folders and the subfolders that you do not even intend to share.

For instance, if your settings are not right and you have overlooked the setting, then you are exposing your personal information to the hackers. Thus, it is recommended that you must not save any of your personal and important information in subfolders of the folders that have been set to "shared" in settings.

In addition, security problems within the P2P program could open the door to attacks from hackers. Some malware is designed to change which folders you have designated for sharing so criminals can access your personal information.

Close Your Connection

There are many occasions where closing the file-sharing program window doesn't actually disconnect you from the network. You feel that you are disconnected from the network, but actually, you are not. Thus, users still have access to the shared files. These things increase the security risk and may slow down your computer. When you are not downloading, just make sure that the program is closed completely.

When you're not downloading files, close the program entirely by doing the following: Double-click on the file-sharing program, choose the file menu, and then choose exit. In addition to that, some of the P2P programs are, by default, open when you turn your computer on. Thus, you need to ensure in start-up menu that these programs are disabled.

Avoid Allowing Multiple Users to Access One Account

Your account might have some information that you do not want others to access or read, but when you allow others to access your account then there is a fair chance that they might access your personal information. Thus, the best solution to this problem is to set up separate user accounts with limited rights. This way you will be the administrator and your control over the computer will increase. No one else will be allowed to install software on your computer. This is one effective strategy that could help you to protect your computer against installing unnecessary software. Moreover, this will also help to limit the access of other users to your personal files. The administrator account should be protected by a strong password. This is important because the password is going to protect unnecessary access to the security features and other rights that you have restricted.

Educate Your Family about File Sharing

If you are a parent, then it is your duty to warn your kids about file-sharing software by letting them know the consequences of this software. You should also hack the devices to ensure whether they have exchanged games, videos, music, or other materials. If they are going to use the software, then let them know the way that software should be installed and used correctly. If you are a teen or a tween, then you need to talk to some elders before using a file-sharing software.

Know the File-Sharing Policies at Work

Your workplace has certain rules about P2P sharing as this can seriously weaken the security of the computer system and expose critical information. To know the details about the business implications of P2P, you should go through the "Peer-to-Peer File Sharing: A Guide for Business" article on the FTC website.

Recovering from a Trojan Horse or Virus

As technology has advanced, our devices have become quite vulnerable to different virus attacks. Even you can face this condition. Since there are huge number of viruses and Trojan horses present on the Internet it is quite astonishing that it didn't happen to you yet. You could have done a better job to protect your computer but that also helps very little because of your current predicament. Once you get an idea that your machine is exhibiting unexpected behavior then you should visit an antivirus website and download a removal tool. There is a fair chance that you might not be able to identify the specific program. Although the other choices available have certain limitations but you could follow the steps written below to protect your files:

1. Call IT support.

   If you have an IT Support Department where you could report the problem then, without wasting a single moment, call them and notify them.

2. Disconnect your computer from the Internet.

   The second thing that you could do is to disconnect your device from the Internet. This is going to help in limiting the access of the one who has attacked your computer. He might use your computer to attack other computers. The best way to accomplish this is to physically disconnect your cable or phone line, but you can also simply disable your network connection.

3. Back up your important files.

   This moment is best to back up your files and the folders so that you do not lose your important files. The best way to do this is to compile your data onto a CD or a DVD or any other external storage device. But you need to note that these files cannot be trusted because these files may also be infected. These files are kept as a backup only to make sure that, if the computer loses everything, the data is not completely lost after recovery.

4. Scan your machine.
    Scanning your computer from a live CD may help to detect the virus. The antivirus already installed on the computer might not help because it may also be infected by the virus. Thus, a live CD may help to catch the virus and remove it safely without deleting any of your personal information or files.

    The next action you will require to have is to install an antivirus software from an unadulterated source such as a USB or a CD. If you do not have one, then you have to choose one from the software available in the market. But the software you chose should provide with the tools you will need. After you have installed the software you should scan the computer. The initial software is going to scan the computer and it might identify the malicious program at the first attempt. The antivirus software is also going to remove the malicious files from your computer. You just need to follow the instructions.

    If your antivirus software locates the virus on your computer then you have to follow the steps written in step 7. In case the antivirus software doesn't detect the malware on your computer then you might have to follow steps 5 and 6.

5. Reinstall your operating system.
    If you are unable to clean your computer from all the above-mentioned steps, then the only option left behind is to install the operating system again. This action is going to result in cleaning all the programs, files, and folders that exist in your computer. It is the only way through which you could get rid of the malware.

    There are a few vendors who offer a rescue partition that is going to allow you to restore your computer to factory defaults. You should check the user manual to ensure whether it offers the rescue partition or not. Before you reinstall, you should make a list of the programs and the settings so that it is easy for you to return your computer to its original condition. You should also make sure that you install the antivirus software again.

6. Restore your files.
If you have made a backup of the files and the folders back in step 3 then you can restore your files from that CD or the storage device. Now, before putting the files and the folders into the computer, scan them with the antivirus software to remove any kind of malware present in them.

7. Protect your computer.
In order to protect your computer from viruses and malware, you should take the following precautions:
- There is no need to open e-mail attachments.
- Avoid following unsolicited links.
- Try to keep your antivirus software updated.
- Use an Internet firewall to protect your computer.
- Make sure your web browser is secure.
- Keep your system patched.

It is important to read articles so that you could ensure that you are protecting your computer in the right way.

Understanding Hidden Threats: Rootkits and Botnets

What are rootkits and botnets?
A rootkit is a piece of software that can be installed on your computer. This is hidden software, and you do not know about it at all. These might come along with the larger software package, or they might get installed by an attacker due to your ignorance over the security of your computer. It is not necessary that rootkits are malicious, but they may hide malicious activities. Through these malicious attacks, the hacker could monitor your actions, modify

programs, or perform other functions on your computer without any of it coming to your knowledge.

Botnet is a combination of two words. The first word is *bot* while the second word that is abbreviated is *network*. Botnet is a program that is completely automated, or it is controlled by a robot. Bots are the computers controlled by one or many others from outside sources. Usually, the attacker gains control by infecting the computer with a virus. Your computer could also be a part of a botnet and you would not even know about it.

Why are they considered threats?

The main problem with botnet and rootkits are that they are hidden. Attackers automatically update them regularly, and your antivirus will not be able to detect them. You can find out about them when you look for a certain activity. Attackers have matured enough; thus they try to make programs that are not detected by antivirus software.

Attackers can use the computer to perform all kinds of illegal activities, such as modifying personal information, attacking other computers, and committing other crimes. Each computer that is a part of a botnet is programmed in such a way that it is able to scan multiple computers for vulnerabilities by monitoring online activity or collecting the information entered in online forms.

What can you do to protect yourself?

You need to practice the following activities to keep your computer secure from rootkits and botnets:

- Try to use the latest and the best antivirus program. This is going to protect your computer against known viruses. Try to update the software regularly so that your computer is not vulnerable to the latest viruses.
- Install a firewall to protect your computer from the types of infection by blocking malicious traffic. This traffic may

enter your computer and limit the traffic you send. Usually, firewalls are included in operating systems, and you just need to make sure they are enabled.

- Use the guidelines for creating a strong password. This way, it will be difficult for the attackers to crack into your account.

- Keep software up-to-date. You should allow the software to automatically update. If you are not able to find the option, then you should regularly watch the vendor's website to look for the updates.

- Follow good security practices so that your computer is safe from the attacks.

- Contact a trained system administrator if you think you are a victim of botnets or rootkits. You may get to know about it when your files are being modified. Using older versions of the files may not prove useful because they will be infected. Thus, the best way is to contact a trained person and ask him to try and recover the data lost.

Vendors are developing software that can detect rootkits and botnets and remove them from your computer. If the software is not able to detect or remove it, then you might have to reinstall the operating system. You may lose the data and the software programs; but if you have maintained a backup, then you can recover from it. Also, the infection may be located at such a deep level that it cannot be removed by simply reinstalling or restoring the operating system. Thus, for that, you have to contact a system administrator.

Understanding Denial-of-Service Attacks

What Is a Denial-of-Service (DoS) attack?
In this type of attack, the attacker is going to attempt to prevent legal users from accessing the information or any of the services available. It will attack your computer through the network connection, and it won't let your computer serve you.

One of the most common DoS attacks happens when the attacker floods the network with information. The website server will be able to process a certain number of requests, but when the hacker will flood the server with requests, then it is going to deny your request. This is known as denial of service because you are not able to utilize the services of the site. Your e-mail account can also be a victim of the same attack. You might be denied use of e-mail service by consuming up all the available services by the hacker.

What Is a Distributed Denial-of-Service (DDoS) Attack?

In this type of attack, your computer is used to launch attacks on other computers. This is called distributed DoS because the hacker is using your computer and many other computers to launch the attack.

How Do You Avoid Being Part of the Problem?

There is no way you could avoid it, but there are ways which can help reduce the chance of becoming a part of it:

- Install and maintain antivirus software.
- Install a firewall.
- Configure the firewall in such a way that restricts the traffic coming into and leaving your computer.
- Follow smart protection activities to make sure that your computer is secure from these attacks.

How Do You Know if an Attack Is Happening?

The following are the symptoms that will let you know if your computer is attacked:

- Unusually slow network performance
- Unavailability of a particular website
- Inability to access any website
- Increase in spam e-mails

What Do You Do if You Think You Are Experiencing an Attack?

The following are the steps that you could take in order to protect your computer from a DoS attack.

- If you are facing a denial of service continuously, then there is a fair chance that you are a victim of DoS. You should contact the network administrator. This may indicate that either your computer or your organization's computer is being attacked.
- Contact your ISP if you are facing the issue on your computer. The ISP will advise you on the right course of action to take.

What Is a Social Engineering Attack?

The social engineering attack is quite different from the above-mentioned attack. This type of attack is made by a person. The aim behind this attack is to get information about an individual or an organization and its computer system. The attacker may demonstrate himself as a customer or an employee or anyone who could gain access to the information. By collecting the information, the attacker could launch an attack on the website of the company.

What Is a Phishing Attack?

Phishing is also a form of social engineering. Phishing attacks are the attacks made through e-mails. The person who sends the e-mails pretends to be a representative of a trustworthy company and asks you to provide personal information. Phishing attacks may also come from other organizations that are involved in charities. Attackers take advantage of natural disasters as well:

- Natural disasters (e.g., Hurricane Katrina, the 2004 Indonesian tsunami)
- Epidemics and health scares (e.g., H1N1)
- Economic concerns (e.g., IRS scams)
- Major political elections

41

- Holidays

How Do You Avoid Being a Victim?

- Do not give your personal information to a person who claims to be a representative from an organization unless or until you completely verify his identity from the company.
- Do not disclose personal information about yourself and your organization.
- Avoid revealing any personal or financial information in e-mails and do not respond to such e-mails that ask for personal information.
- Do not send personal or sensitive information over an unsecure network.
- Make sure there is an *s* in https as this ensures that the website is secure. Malicious websites may have the same name but with a different domain extension. Make sure that this is the right website.
- Contact the company to verify if the e-mail is legitimate or not.
- Install good and updated antivirus software, firewalls, and e-mail filters to secure your computer.
- Try to take advantage of anti-phishing activities offered online.

What Do You Do if You Think You Are a Victim?

- Report it to the appropriate person immediately and ask for guidelines.
- If your financial information is compromised, then you should contact the bank or credit card company to immediately block services and change online passwords.
- Immediately change passwords of all the online services that you use.
- Compare the signs of identity theft.
- Report the attack on http://www.ftc.gov/.

Socializing Securely: Using Social Networking Services

Social Networking Serves Many Purposes

Social networking websites provide an opportunity for people to connect and share information. There are millions and thousands of people across the world that regularly access these sites to share different statuses, pictures, and other important stuff. Some of the renowned and reliable surveys show that there are more than five hundred million active users on Facebook, 175 million registered users on Twitter, more than one hundred million users on MySpace, and more than eighty million members on LinkedIn.

These websites provide people with a way to connect to each other even while sitting miles apart. These sites are available on mobile devices as well thus they have become quite widespread in this modern age. There are several different reasons due to which these websites are used. The following are the reasons due to which the use of these websites has increased:

- To network with new contacts
- Reconnect with former friends
- Maintain current relationships
- Build or promote a business or project
- Participate in discussions or forums that are made on a certain topic
- Fun and entertainment purposes

There are several social networking websites such as Facebook and Twitter. These sites have a wide range of users because each of these websites offers different services. For instance, there are a lot of members on LinkedIn because it is a professional networking site.

Sharing Information Presents Risks

There are certain risks involved in sharing information online. Thus, you need to know the potential risks involved in sharing information online.

Attacks and Unintended Information Disclosure

Attackers use social networking websites to spread malicious code and this is going to compromise your computer and access personal or sensitive information. You may also reveal information to unauthorized individuals. The following are some of the most common threats you face on social networking sites:

Viruses. Social networking websites are an ideal place for the attackers to get personal and other sensitive information. An attacker can create a virus and embed it into an application or a website, thus affecting millions of computers.

Tools. Attackers may use tools that allow them to take control of a user's account. With the help of these tools, attackers can get access to a user's personal data and other sensitive information. Attackers can also post malicious content through your account.

Social engineering attacks. These types of attacks are done by people who steal different information from others and perform some illegal actions. They may even post such content on your account that may result in other computers also getting infected with it.

Identity theft. People may steal your identity and they may practice different illegal actions. This way you will be held accountable for the acts even though you do not know what you actually did.

Third-party applications. Social networking sites may also ask you to download some third-party applications such as games and/or quizzes that will provide additional functionality. These applications might not involve malicious content, but they will access your personal information and they might use it in the wrong way.

Professional and Personal Implications

The information you post on these sites may also present an amount of risk to your professional opportunities, personal relationships, and safety.

Business data. Posting business data that is confidential may result in serious consequences. The company whose information you disclose might sue you for disclosing information about customers, intellectual property, human resource issues, mergers and acquisitions, or other company activities. This information will be useful for the attackers and even for the competitors in the market.

Professional reputation. Sharing inappropriate information may result in losing good reputation. Universities and colleges might search for potential students on these sites. Thus, these acts might work negatively on your side. Sharing inappropriate information may suggest that people might be unreliable, untrustworthy, or unprofessional and it may result in disqualification. There are certain cases of people losing jobs because of the inappropriate content they share.

Personal relationships. Inappropriate content can also affect your personal relationships. Since these websites can be accessed by anyone around thus they may post such comments or pictures that may affect the emotions of another.

PERSONAL SAFETY

Your personal safety may also be compromised when you join these social websites. By posting pictures or revealing your location, you are making yourself vulnerable to physical attack.

One important factor that needs to be talked about here is that people usually share information about others without even knowing that this may put them in danger. Sometimes, posting negative content about someone else is intentional. Social networking services have become channels for conducting cyber bullying—a growing problem that can lead to significant psychological trauma.

Proceed with Caution
Social networking websites are quite useful and you can spend a good time on them, but it is extremely important to take proper steps to protect your personal information from being compromised.

Implement Security Measures
Some of the most effective general security protections are:

- Use strong passwords and do not repeat passwords.
- Keep antivirus software up-to-date.
- Update your software as soon as the update is released.

Follow Good Practices
There are some unique risks involved in social networking services, but you have the opportunity to minimize these risks by following the below mentioned practices:

1. You should use strong privacy and security settings. You should change your privacy and security settings periodically so that you are safe from such attacks. The privacy settings are periodically updated, thus you also need to review them and look for changes and ensure that you have the right option selected.
2. Avoid using third party applications as they might be unsecure.
3. Try to use only those applications that are developed by trustworthy vendors. Avoid using applications that seem suspicious.
4. Do not trust anyone and treat everything as public. The best way to protect yourself is by limiting the amount of personal information you post on the social networking sites.

5. Share information only to the ones you trust. This way your information will not get into the wrong hands and it will be kept private. Usually, young people give away their personal information to make friends online. But that is totally wrong because, this way, they might be involved in identity theft.

You need to be responsible if you want to save yourself from these attacks because the software can only protect you up to a certain level.

Chapter 4

DISPOSING OF OLD DEVICES

Almost every year, you can find numerous new computer models in the market. You can ensure that the hard drive is disposed of completely. Otherwise, it may become a treasure chest for identity thieves. Thus, before selling your computer, you need to make sure that you use a program that overwrites or wipes all the information off the hard drive many times. If you can't do it, then remove the hard drive and destroy it physically.

Get To Know Your Hard Drive
Usually, computers store personal and financial information like
- Passwords
- Account Numbers
- License Keys for paid software programs or their registration numbers
- Personal Addresses
- Phone Numbers
- Medical Reports and Prescription Information
- Your personal or family's tax returns
- Important files created by the browser and operating system.

When you save a large file, it is scattered around the hard drive in bits and pieces. When you request the computer to open the file, it gathers the bits and pieces together and presents a complete file in front of you.

When you delete files, the file actually remains on your computer. Only the link required to reconstruct the file has disappeared. The bits and pieces remain on your computer unless or until they are overwritten. These files and folders can be retrieved through a data recovery program. In order to completely remove the contents of the hard drive, you need to wipe out the hard drive.

How to Clean a Hard Drive
You must have some important information on your hard drive that you do not want to wipe out so it is better to save those files on one of the following so that your data is safe:

o USB drive
o CD-ROM
o An external hard drive
o Hard drive of your new computer

You need to check the user manual or the manufacturer's website to get to know the information required to save the data and transfer it to the new computer. The programs that help to do these small tasks are known as utility programs. There are certain utility programs available in stores and on the Internet for free that wipe out the hard drive. These programs are usually inexpensive and they vary a lot.

o Some programs are meant to erase the entire disk while others allow you to select certain files or folders to erase.
o Some programs are built to overwrite or wipe out the hard drive many times while others overwrite or wipe out only once.

You need to consider using a program that overwrites or wipes the hard drive many times so that this way there is no chance that your information could be retrieved. The other solution to this problem is to remove the hard drive and physically destroy it.

If you are using your company's computer for home purpose, then you need to check with the company's rules and regulations about the way to manage the information that's business related on your computer.

Certain Ways to Dispose Of Your Computers

There are several different ways to dispose of the computers and here under this subheading we are going to discuss them.

Recycle It

There are several computer manufacturers who have certain programs to recycle the computer and their components. So, when disposing of your computer, you need to check their websites and call their toll-free numbers for collecting the information. You can get information about electronic product recycling programs from the Environmental Protection Agency (EPA).

Your local community will have the recycling program as well. Check out with your country or local government. You should also check with the local landfill office for regulations.

Donate It

There are several such organizations that take computers and then use it for charities.

Resell It

There are several such organizations that buy old computers. Thus, you may even resell your computer to a company who deals in old laptops.

One aspect that needs to be understood and remembered while disposing of computers is that computers are made of different metals that may contaminate the earth. Thus, EPA recommends that you first check out with the local health and sanitation department to get to know about the ways to dispose of computers safely without harming the earth.

Disposing of Your Mobile Device

You can now get a new mobile phone model almost every year. But what happens to the old one if you want to upgrade to a new mobile phone? You definitely have to dispose of the first one. But it is extremely important to delete the personal information stored on your phone.

Ways to Remove Personal Information

Your mobile device holds sensitive information like addresses and phone numbers, account numbers, e-mail, voice mail, and text message logs. Thus, it is extremely important to take the necessary steps when you have to get rid of your old device to ensure that your personal information doesn't get into the wrong hands.

The first step is to use the factory data reset. There are numerous devices that offer this particular option as they wipe out your device and clear nearly all the information in its memory. There are a few names that describe this option. Some may call it hard reset or some may call it factory reset. But you need to transfer your information to your new device before you delete it from your old one. You must have a user manual that will describe how to reset your device.

The second option is to remove or erase the SD cards and the SIM card. SIM cards can store important contact information and SD cards can store your other data like songs, files, and much more. You need to ask your service provider to transfer your SIM to the new device. When you wipe out your device through factory reset

51

your SD Card and the SIM card retains the data. You can remove the SD card before removing or disposing of the phone.

Checking Twice

After deleting the personal information, you need to double check your phone to make sure that all the information is gone. You need to check the following things:

- Your phone book to check if all contacts are removed
- Call log is completely empty
- All voice mails are empty
- Sent and received text messages and e-mails are completely removed
- Download folder is empty
- Search histories are removed completely
- Personal photos are removed completely

The trend of smartphones has allowed the users to download and install numerous apps to assist them on the go. These apps have certain information stored on them. Thus, it is highly important to delete that information.

Discarding with Care

Now your phone is clean to go wherever it wants. You have to decide now what to do next with this piece of electronic device.

The first option that comes to mind is recycling. There are numerous companies out there that have programs to refurbish mobile devices or recycle their components including accessories like chargers. To get to information about recycling you may visit the websites of the following companies:

- The Environmental Protection Agency (EPA)
- CTIA—The Wireless Association
- The carrier you are currently using

The other option to dispose of your device is to donate your device. There are several such companies who collect used phones for charitable purposes.

You can even trade in a new device for the old one. This way you will get some amount that you can use to buy the new device. You can even dispose of the device, but before doing that you need to keep the environment in mind. The EPA recommends that you check with your local health and sanitation agencies for their preferred way to dispose of electronics.

Chapter 5

Understanding Mobile Apps

If you have a smartphone then you must have some apps that will allow you to play games, get turn by turn directions, and access many other services. These apps are easy to download and most apps are free. These apps are so much fun and they provide a lot of convenience. You download these apps without even thinking about the key considerations like how they're paid for, what information they may gather from your device, or who gets that information.

Mobile App Basics

What's a Mobile App?
A mobile app is a software program that you can download on your mobile phone or tablet. You can access the application directly using your phone or other mobile device.

What Do I Need to Download and Use an App?
To download the apps, you need to have a mobile device and access to the Internet. Not all the apps work on all mobile devices. Once you buy a device you need to be committed to use the operating system that it provides and the apps that go along with it. Some of the most famous operating systems currently residing in the market are Android, Apple, Microsoft and BlackBerry mobile operating systems. This operating system has an app store where

you can search for the app and download and install it. There are a few retailers who also offer app stores but you have to make sure that app store works with your operating system. You have to set up an account where you have to provide credit card information, especially if you are going to download an app that is not free.

Data Plans and Wi-Fi

Two of the most common ways to access the Internet is either to use your carrier services or to use Wi-Fi. You have to pay the phone company's monthly fee for the data plan you use. Wi-Fi connections are usually much faster than data plans but, to utilize Wi-Fi, you have to be within the range of the device. You can find Wi-Fi in coffee shops, airports, and many other public places, but these networks do not encrypt data thus they are not secure enough to share confidential information.

To set up a home wireless network you'll need to pay for Internet access and a wireless router, and you'll want to take steps to secure the network.

Why are some apps free?

Have you ever wondered how developers would earn if they are going to provide apps free of cost? The following are some of the ways these developers earn:

- Some of the developers sell advertising space within the apps. The app developers can earn money from the ads so they try to reach as many users as possible.
- Some of the developers offer basic versions for free and then they ask their customers to buy the premium version with extensive features.
- Some apps allow the customers to buy in-app features. Usually, you are billed for these in-app purchases through the credit card information stored in your app store account. There are devices that have the option to block in-app purchases.

- There are a few apps that are offered free to make you interested in the company's other product. The sole purpose of these apps is to advertise that product.

Questions About Your Privacy
What Types of Data Can Apps Access?

When you sign up on the app store or download an app from the app store then you might be asked for permission to allow them access to the information on your device. The information accessed by some of the apps is as follows:

- Phone contact
- E-mail contact
- Call logs
- Internet data
- Calendar data
- Device location
- Device unique ID or MAC address
- Your opinion about the app

When you are providing the necessary information there is someone on the other end who is receiving this information. The collector might be the app developer, the app store, an advertiser, or an ad network. They collect your data and share it with other companies.

How can I tell what information an app will access or share?

It is not an easy way to know what data a particular app will access or the way it will be used. So it is important that, when you download an app, you consider what you know about who created it and what it will do. You must also go through the information about the developer. You can get the information about the app through the app store. But it depends upon the developer if they will provide the information. If they do, then you will be able to access it and probably, this way, you might get to know whether the app is trustworthy or not.

If you are an Android user, then you will be allowed to read the permissions just before you install the app. You should go through them. That information will contain the details of the information the app is going to access on your device. You need to ask yourself whether the permissions make sense or not. For instance, if you are downloading an e-book, then why would they ask you for permission to access your messages?

Why Is Location Data So Important for Some Apps?
There are some apps that are useless without your current location. The reason is that these apps are meant to assist you, and your location is the basic requirement for them. For instance, Google Maps is almost useless if your current location is not available in the app. There are some apps that provide your location data to ad networks, which will combine it with other information in their database to target ads based on your interest and your location.

If you have allowed the app to access your location, then it is going to access your location until you change the settings on your phone. If you are not willing to share the location on your phone, then you have the liberty to change the location settings from the settings tab. If you have changed location services in your settings then the apps won't be able to give you information based on your location unless or until you manually enter the location. The general data about your phone is used to judge the location of the phone as the phone carrier has to efficiently route calls.

Your phone uses general data about its location so your phone carrier can efficiently route calls. Even if you turn off location services in your phone's settings, it may not be possible to completely stop it from broadcasting your location data.

Questions About Advertising
Why Does the App I Downloaded Have Ads in It?
The developers intend to make inexpensive apps so that people do not hesitate when buying apps. If they earn money by selling the

advertising space, then the app might cost less. Some developers sell the space to the networks, who ultimately sell space to advertisers.

Why Do I See the Ads I Do?

Developers have to earn money through something; thus if they do not charge from you, they are selling space on the app to the advertising networks. Advertisers believe that you are quite likely to click on the ad targeted to your specific interest. Thus, these ad networks gather information that even includes your location data, and they might combine it with the kind of information you provide when you register for a service or buy something online. The combined information will allow the networks to send you targeted ads.

Malware and Security Concerns

Should I Update My Apps?

Your phone will indicate when the apps need an update. It is quite a good idea to update apps because the apps are going to add new and exciting features into themselves. These updates usually contain security patches that will help to protect your information and even your device from viruses and malware.

Could an App Infect My Phone with Malware?

Yes, definitely, as there are some hackers who create an app with the intent to infect phones with malware. You will get to know that your phone has a virus or a malware if it sends messages and e-mails that you haven't written. The malware could also download apps on your phone all by itself.

If you have doubts that you have a malware on your phone, then you can perform the following steps:

- Contact customer support
- Contact your mobile carrier for help
- Install a security app like an antivirus software

You might not be able to find lots of security apps for mobile because they are newly introduced. Those which are there to service will scan your phone and remove malware if detected.

Mobile App User Reviews
Should We Believe the User Reviews?
User reviews are an effective way to find out if the app will prove to be useful or not. But nowadays a lot of developers and the people responsible for their marketing have posed as consumers and posted positive reviews on the apps. These reviews are not realistic because they are posted majorly by those who have made the app. The Federal Trade Commission found a company posting fake reviews on the apps thus it was sued.

Kids and Mobile Apps
What Elements Should I Be Aware of Before Downloading the App for My Kids?
FTC staff found out through a recent survey that kids' apps might

- have the ability to collect and share personal information;
- allow your kid to spend real money, disregarding the fact that the app is free;
- and the app should include ads and link to the social media apps.

The Things That Apps Are Doing but Are Hidden From You
Before downloading an app, you need to look into the description of the app and view the screen shots, view the content rating, and the user reviews so that you get an idea of what type of app you are downloading. Search the Internet for the reviews of that particular app.
Are There Ways to Restrict How My Kids Use Apps?
Yes, there are certain ways to restrict the use of apps. Before you hand over your smart device into the hands of your kid, make sure that you have gone through the settings. You should make sure that you have restricted the content that is not right for your kid.

You can set up a password so that your kid can't buy apps or even be able to download apps. You can even turn off the Wi-Fi in the settings or manually turn off the Wi-Fi so that they cannot access the Internet all by themselves. The most effective way to keep kids away from malware is to educate them about it. You should talk with them about the rules for using the apps.

Apps to Help You Shop in Stores

If you have a good shopping buddy who has a sharp eye, is well aware of the lay of the land, and can find the best deals on the products you want, then it is a blessing. He may even share coupons with you. There are millions of people who find new shopping buddies in their smartphones.

What Can Shopping Apps Do?

The following are the features that you are going to find in shopping apps:

In-store purchases

These are the apps that allow using and buying the features within the app. You can pay for the apps through the QR code that is the quick response code or the barcode. When you intend to spend money on in-store purchases, then you can pay by tapping your phone against an electronic reader.

In order to fund your in-store purchases, you need to link your app store account to your credit card, debit card, gift card, or prepaid card. There are a few apps that are known as pass-through apps. These are the apps that charge your bank account each time you buy something.

Some of the other apps allow you to store a value within the app, and you spend from that particular stored value every time you buy anything from something.

Price comparison

These apps are going to help you compare the prices of different products in real time. Several apps use your phone camera to scan the code of the product. Then they search the online database so that they could show you the pictures and prices available on the Internet.

Deals

These apps are also helpful in many ways. These apps are going to help you find, earn, or redeem coupons or loyalty points. You can use these things when you shop in-store. Some apps also offer a special discount based on the information they collect from your phone—such as your location, purchase history, and much more.

There are several such apps that combine these features. For instance, there are some retailers that provide the option of in-store purchases, and the same apps also offer coupons for their products.

What Should One Do If They Discover a Billing Error or Unauthorized Charge When They Use an In-Store Purchase App?

If you think that there is something wrong with the payment, just report it to the app store or the app or the credit or debit card linked to the app.

The Store

It is possible to solve payment issues by talking to the store employees. But you need to make sure that you talk to them as soon as possible because there is a certain time limit for returns and refunds. If you use an app that is developed by the retailer then the employees will definitely help you out with the issues you face.

In case the first employee is unable to help you out, then you need to ask your supervisor or the manager. You need to explain each and every problem in detail and request them to fix it for you. You should keep a record of the conversations.

The App

An FTC study states that the user agreements for shopping apps generally offers few promises that the app company will help out in case of any problem. While there are some user agreements that also claim that the app company doesn't take any kind of responsibility for any problem. The company might not be rude to customers, but there is no guarantee that they are going to help anyway.

Some aspects that you need to look for before purchasing are:
- The contact information
- The time period in which you could report unauthorized changes
- The boundaries defined on your responsibility for unauthorized charges
- How quickly the company will respond with the results of your claim

You can review this information in the app help section, frequently asked questions, or terms of use.

The Credit or Debit Card
If the in-store purchase app falls in the category of pass-through apps, then the following are the legal protections that can be applied to your debit or credit cards.

Table 1: Responsibility for Unauthorized Charges Fluctuates by Payment Method

Payment Method	According to the law, you are responsible for an unauthorized charge is limit of:
Credit card	$50
Debit card	$50 Only if you report within two days of discovery. $500 If you report within two business days, but within the time period of sixty days after you receive your statement which shows the issue. All the charges if you do not report within sixty days after you receive the statement which demonstrates the issue.
Gift cards, virtual currency, or money stored in an app	There is no fixed limit on your liability. You are the one responsible for all the charges. You could be saved only through one condition and that is if the gift card conditions state that you will not be held responsible.

If you use an app that uses a stored-value procedure, then you might not be protected as you are protected in credit or debit cards. Before using a stored-value app, just go through the app description or the user agreement to get to know the way the payment works and what will happen if there is an issue. If you are unable to find that information, try to use a different app or keep the stored value up to a limit that you could afford.

What Personal Information Do Shopping Apps Collect?

There are some shopping apps that collect your location data so that they could send you the discount messages through a text message or a push notification when you are near a relevant business. Shopping apps also collect other information as well such as your e-mail, phone number, name, and much more. Some apps ask for your personal information that may include your Social Security number, driver's license number, date of birth, and gender. For such apps, you need to consider whether the convenience of the app is worth the risks that sensitive information is stored or shared by the app developer.

When you make a transaction with a company, then all the records are joined with your personal profile. Usually, companies sell this data to the advertisers, brokers, or credit reporting companies. Thus, you need to look for companies that promise the user to keep their private information secure. There are several such apps in the market, and they live up to their promise. If they do not, then you can report to the FTC.

Chapter 6

GUIDE FOR ONLINE AUCTIONS

Online auction sites offer a lot for the buyers. Auction sites not only provide you ease of getting the item while sitting back home but also allow you to sell items as well. But before you commit to any buyer or seller, you need to first check out the site, the seller operating behind it, and the scams that may crop in. This way, you will have a better experience on these sites.

Get to know how the site works

These sites have rules and regulations for both buyers and sellers. Thus, before you perform an action, you need to go through these rules and regulations.

- Payment Methods
  Do you have the liberty to pay through safe payment methods like credit cards that come with fraud protection?

- Privacy and security
  Go through the site protection rules and regulations. Make sure the pages you visit are encrypted and where you register as a buyer or seller is also secure.

- Disputes
  Ensure that, in case of a dispute, the site will be able to resolve the issue with the seller.

You need to go through the complaints and reviews of the existing users. You will be able to find them on Google.

Check out the item

Before buying an item from the auction site, just spare some time to research for the product online. There are several sites that will offer the product. This way, you will be able to get to know about the price of the product.

When you scroll through the site, you should look closely at the photos and read the description carefully. For instance:

- The photos of the product show the same product that you have bid for. If the ad has generic photos, then you are sure that the seller has the item.
- If the item description has the words *refurbished, vintage, used,* or *closeout,* then there is a fair chance that the item is not top-notch.
- If the brand name is shown with a low price, then it is definitely a fraud.

Check out the seller

You should look for a seller that accepts safer payment methods like credit cards, a secure online payment method, or an escrow service that is recommended by the auction site. Avoid doing business with the ones who accept money transfer, cash or wire transfers, or reloadable cards. This way, you will not be able to get back the money.

You should also check the seller's rating on the site and read the comments to get to know if the seller is reliable or not. You can judge this by the comments of recent buyers. If you are comfortable with the seller, then trust your gut and bid on the item.

Read the seller's contact information and ensure that it includes an e-mail. If you are not satisfied with the description, just e-mail the seller for inquiry. If you are not satisfied with the reply or you do not get a response, then you should move on.

Every seller has his own way of doing business. You must ensure before bidding that the seller gives you the right to return or gives product warranty. It should be mentioned in the product listing. You may also want to know

- if the item has a warranty or not and the time period of the warranty.
- what the shipping options are and who is responsible for paying the shipping dues. (You must calculate the shipping costs before you bid as this will help to avoid a costly surprise later.)
- the return or exchange conditions.

When you bid and pay

Before bidding, decide the amount you are willing to spend as there are "shill bidders" who have the intention to raise the price, but they are not serious buyers. Thus, stick to the amount you say as your cost will add up with the other costs, such as shipping, handling, taxes, or to receive or return the item.

If you are the highest bidder, then try and save the copies of the item description and the final price. Pay for the item through credit card or through a reliable money transfer service like escrow.

When you pay through a credit card, the Fair Credit Billing Act will protect your transaction. It allows you to dispute charges under some circumstances and temporarily withhold payment while the creditor investigates.

How to work out problems

If you do not receive the item as per the description or the item doesn't arrive by the date promised, then the first thing you need to do is to contact the seller. According to the FTC rule a seller is bound to ship the item on the date promised or within thirty days after the date ordered if no date was promised. If the seller is unable to help, then you need to seek help from the auction site. You do not want to wait so long for the seller that you miss the deadline of the site.

If you have paid through a credit card, then you can inform the credit card company and withhold the payment while the company investigates about the matter. If you see any charges you do not recognize in your credit card statement, immediately inquire about it from the credit card company.

Avoiding scams
Be careful of the scammers online as they are not interested in offering bargains because they are only interested in money and your personal information.

Avoid clicking *Reply* or clicking on links in an e-mail message
If it looks like a message from the auction site or online payment site and you are given a link, just do not click on the links given. The reason being that you might end up on a spoof site and you may either lose your personal information or download malware into your computer. The following are some of the most common examples of e-mails you may get:

- "Your account will be shut down if you don't respond immediately to validate your information."
- "Reply to confirm your account number and payment or you'll lose the item you bid on."
- "We suspect an unauthorized transaction on your account; click here to verify your account details."

To check if that is true, you need to log in to the auction site and check your notifications. If you have actually received a notification there, then you can trust the e-mail; otherwise, it is a scam.

You should communicate only through the auction and payment site. Avoid deals with people who want to pay you through some other payment system. If you agree to use any other payment methods, then you may lose the protection the site provides. You might lose the payment and the product as well. Here's an example of how a contact might start:

- A scammer may ask you to e-mail him outside the auction site by claiming that he was the highest bidder who backed out. He may request you to give him a second chance and he may even offer to pay a good price for the product. He doesn't want to involve the auction site in between and wants to close the deal through a wire transfer.

- You are the one who has placed the highest bid and seller requests you to pay him through the payment method he opts for. He might make up a story to prove that the online payment system doesn't work for you. This means that he is scamming you and he just wants money from you, and you will not get any product.

Report fraud
If you are facing some issues with an online transaction, try to ensure that you work them out directly with the seller and the auction site. If it doesn't work out for you that way, then contact the Federal Trade Commission and your attorney general.

Ways to Be Smart Online
The Internet makes numerous tasks easier, faster, and more convenient such as shopping which has now become a lot easier than before. Before the invention of the Internet, people had to go to the libraries to look for information, but now, in this modern age, they could research for the product easily. It has provided a lot more convenience in communication as well. The only thing you need to do is to get tips for being safe and making your time online a lot more useful.

Online Auctions for Sellers

If you have items to sell quickly and you do not have time to go to the market and sell them, the best way to do this is to sell them online. Before posting the ad, you need to check the responsibilities, the best practices, and the ways to spot scams so that your time online is not a waste.

Choose a Site

You need to choose a website that fulfills all your needs. The best way to choose a site is to check

- if you like to shop at that online store,
- what you need to become a seller and whether the amount you are demanding is reasonable or not,
- your compatibility with site rules and regulations,
- if the site offers help like it provides instructions or ideas about best practices for creating your account page, writing listings, or managing your business;
- the site is helpful in communicating with buyers,
- reviews of current sellers about the website,
- the ways you will be getting paid. Different sites use different payment methods some of which are secure while others are not. You need to check if it allows the opportunity to use credit cards or not. If you want to sell out an expensive good then you must use services like PayPal or escrow service,
- if your information is secure. You will have to provide your personal information like your credit card information or account number thus you have to ensure that the website is secure.

List an Item

You need to add honest details of your product. Be realistic about the product and the price. If you are going to add fake details then there is a fair chance that you will be disallowed to post an ad or people might give negative reviews about you. You need to add photos in your ad too so that the user can see the condition of your product.

Explain How You Operate

Your rules and policies can affect one's bidding decisions. Thus, it is extremely important that your policies are easy to find and clear enough so that they could be understood at first attempt.

- Types of payment methods you accept
- Does the item come with a guarantee? If yes, then how long will the warranty last and what does it cover?
- Tell clearly if you accept tax returns and exchanges or not
- The shipping options you offer and the one who is responsible for paying it

You need to be aware of the deadlines. The FTC rule states that you need to ship the items sold within the time limit you state or, at maximum, within thirty days. If you do not fulfill the commitment then you have to agree to a new date or cancel the order for a full refund.

Keep Transaction Records

You need to keep track of all the transactions you have made. Your transaction details should keep track of the product description, final price, and your communication with the buyer. You need to keep the auction or payment system details as well.

The Internal Revenue Service (IRS) has a small business website where you could find the information about the recordkeeping requirements for online auction sellers, whether they sell occasionally or as an ongoing business. The guide explains that you need to keep a record of sensitive information like customer name, customer ID, etc.

Work Out Problems

It is extremely important to keep records of transactions because it will prove useful if there is a customer complaint about an item's quality or features or to check whether the package arrived on time or not. If you both are not able to resolve the issue then you should go to the site dispute resolution staff and explain all the details with proof and demand for their help.

Scams Against Sellers

Scammers are not concerned with the price you are paying. They are just concerned with the personal information, money, and your merchandise. There are certain steps you need to take to guard against them. You should use safe and reliable payment methods so that the scammers do not get a chance to scam you. You should either use credit cards or escrow service as they are the most reliable.

Use Safer Payment Methods

It's a big risk if you are accepting a cashier's check or money order because it will take a while to reveal that the check or the money order is a fraud. If you ship out the product before the check or money order is fully cleared, then you are risking the product.

Don't rely on customers who ask for your account number because, once the buyer gets the account number, he will take your money instead of adding it. When the buyer requests for your account number, you need to be extra careful as it can be a fraud. You need to either report it or request for him to pay through a more reliable way.

Check online for all other reliable payment companies. You also need to research fully about escrow as well. Just type the name in Google search and write the word *complaint* and *review* and see whether this service is reliable and fits your situation or not. Just make it clear to the buyer that you should receive the payment from escrow. If you get an e-mail from some other company then make sure if it is a prank and you are being scammed. Just do not ship the product on the basis of that e-mail because, this way, you will lose money and the product.

Log Out of Your Account

If you get e-mails from sites that say that you have received a payment and get a link in the e-mail then avoid opening the link or replying to the e-mail because they are a spam. Although the message you will receive will be quite intimidating. Some of the common examples of the message would be as follows:

- "Your account will be shut down if you don't respond immediately to validate your information."
- "We suspect an unauthorized transaction on your account; click here to verify your account details."

The basic intention of the scammer would be to steal your information or trick you to download malware on your computer. Instead of replying to that particular e-mail, just confirm from the auction or payment site if they have sent you a notification or not. You can reply to that notification there and it will be more reliable to respond there.

The scammer might e-mail you from the company that you want them to pay from. The e-mail might look the same as the original, but it will not be. To confirm whether it is authentic, just log into that auction site and check your account for the payment.

Sell the Items in Your Possession

In a prolonged scheme, a scammer usually contacts the seller and requests him to list down his items for him and collect payment from the buyer. The scammer will request the seller to keep a share of the payment and forward the rest of the payment to him. The scammer even lies that he will send the merchandise directly to the buyer. Since the person in between is a fraud, the buyer will not get the product and the seller is not going to receive the payment. In the end, the buyer is going to demand a refund and make a complaint against you.

Contact the Buyer through the Contact Information Provided
If some reliable bidder contacts you and asks you to ship your merchandise to the address that is not listed on the account, then there is definitely something wrong. He must be a scammer who hijacked the real bidder's account, and now he is offering sellers to send their product to him. Just use the contact information on the website given and protect yourself and the true buyer.

Inform the Site about the Buyer
You need to inform the site about the scam immediately. For instance, if the buyer asks for a refund and sends you junk instead of the real product, then you need to immediately inform the site operators.

Report Fraud
If you face issues during online auction transactions, try to work out directly with the buyer and the auction site. If it doesn't work, request assistance from the Federal Trade Commission and your state attorney general.

Chapter 7

TIPS FOR USING PUBLIC
WI-FI NETWORKS

Usually, the Wi-Fi available in coffee shops, libraries, airports, hotels, universities, and other public places is not secure. That is why people avoid sharing important information through these networks. The information sent over an insecure network can easily be accessed by someone else.

In order to protect the information on wireless hot spots, you should send information only to a site that is fully encrypted. You should even avoid using mobile apps that require personal or financial information.

How Encryption Works
Encryption is responsible for keeping your personal information secure online. Encryption works by scrambling the information you send over the Internet. It converts your data into a code that cannot be accessed by others. While using a wireless network, ensure that you send the data over an encrypted network. An encrypted network ensures that all the data sent through that particular network is secure.

How to Tell If a Website is Encrypted
Have you ever imagined where your information goes to when you share files over the Internet? Actually, these files are stored on

the server, which is a powerful computer that collects and delivers content. Banking websites and other websites that have to deal with money and personal information use encryption to guard the information while it travels from a server to a computer.

To check if the website is encrypted, you have to check if it has the *s* in *https*—which is located at the start of the website address. There are several such websites that use encryption only on sign-in pages. You need to avoid giving out your information to such websites because the parts of sessions that are not encrypted are going to make all your personal information vulnerable.

What About Mobile Apps?
When you work with websites there is a visible indicator for whether the website is encrypted or not but mobile apps don't have a visible indicator. It has been found out by researchers that there are several websites that do not use encryption properly. Thus, it is highly risky to use certain mobile apps on unsecured networks. You should use a secure network to make sensitive transactions.

Another option would be to use the company's website instead of using the company's mobile app. This way you will also get to know that the company's website is secure by checking the start of the website address.

Don't Assume a Wi-Fi Hot spot is Secure
There are several Wi-Fi hot spots that are unsecure. If the network requires a WPA or WPA2 password, then the network is secure.

If you use a network that is insecure and log in to an unencrypted website then your information is vulnerable to attack. Hackers could easily hijack your session and they may log in with your sign-in information. Your personal information and other important documents will be up for grab.

There are several new hacking tools available on the Internet for free. These tools help hackers to easily crack the information even if the person using the software is not tech savvy.

When an imposter will log in to your account he will impersonate you and he may even scam the people in your contact list. It is also possible that the hacker may use your information to access other websites. He may even access those websites that may contain your financial information.

Protect Your Information When Using Public Wi-Fi
The following are some of the most useful ways through which you could protect your information;

- When you are using a hot spot, make sure you send information to sites that are fully encrypted. You also need to ensure that each and every page of the website is encrypted. If you find a page without the *s* in *https* then just immediately log out of the network.
- Try to log out from the accounts after you have used them.
- Avoid using the same password on different websites. This way, if one of your account gets hacked, not all your accounts will be vulnerable to attack.
- Pay attention to browser alerts and act accordingly.
- Change the settings of your mobile device so that it doesn't connect automatically to the Wi-Fi nearby.
- If you regularly access online accounts through the Wi-Fi hot spots, then try using a VPS that is going to encrypt the traffic between your computer and the Internet. This is also going to work on unsecured networks. VPN is also available for mobile devices as well.
- Ensure that the Wi-Fi uses WPA2 to protect your information as it is the strongest. There are some Wi-Fi that use WEP and WPA encryption that may not protect you against hacking issues.
- You should install browser add-ons and plug-ins to help you protect the data. Force-TLS and HTTPS Everywhere

are powerful add-ons found in Mozilla that force the browser to use encryption on popular websites that usually aren't encrypted. They do not protect you from all kinds of website thus it's important that you look for *https* in the URL.

- You also need to take necessary steps to ensure that your wireless network is secure.

Chapter 8

USING IP CAMERAS SAFELY

Network or Internet cameras are usually promoted as IP cameras. These cameras prove quite useful for keeping an eye on your property, your family, and even your pets. The camera provides you with audio and video feeds that you can access remotely using your Internet browser. But these IP cameras are vulnerable to digital snooping.

Before Buying an IP Camera

The IP camera allows you to monitor the place where you have it fixed. It could be your house or your business. It uses particular software that connects you directly to the Internet. It is different from a webcam because it doesn't require you to transmit a video online. But if your IP camera is not encrypting the information it is sending, then there is a fair chance that someone might snoop in. Thus, while shopping for IP cameras, you have to put the security feature on top of your list.

Secure Wireless Transmission

The IP camera sends the whole feed to the wireless router. If you have a good wireless security protocol, then it will help you secure your video feed during the time it is travelling to the router. You should buy a camera that supports WPA2.

Secure Internet Transmission

If you want to access your camera's video feed remotely, then your camera will be responsible to send the information beyond the wireless router over the Internet. Not all the cameras are going to provide you with the same level of security for this. You need to buy a camera that encrypts the information. The camera you buy must use SSL/TLS, or some other industry standard, to protect your information. If the camera uses the above-mentioned security credentials, then it will also encrypt the website in which you log in.

Multiple Users

If you want more than one person to keep a check on your home or on the business, then you should buy a camera that gives you the option to have different levels of access. For example, you will have the administrator access while the others would only be able to view what is going on.

Using Security Features

Now, if you have bought your camera, make sure you set it up with security features. The following are the details that are going to help you set up your camera:

Make Sure to Keep the Software Up-to-Date

The software that comes along with your camera is updated by the manufacturer frequently. Thus, it is important to check if the website offers an updated version of the software. If it does, then install the updated version. You also need to ensure that you have the right settings that will allow the software to update automatically.

Check Your Camera's Password Settings

There are several such IP cameras that allow you to turn off the camera password requirement. If you will turn off the option, your video feed will be a lot more vulnerable to attacks.

Use a Strong Password

You should choose a strong password for your IP camera so that it is difficult for the hacker to get access. Make sure you change the default username and the password as these defaults are publicly known.

Enable Your Camera's Security Features

Make sure you enable the entire required security feature. If your camera gives you the opportunity to turn the encryption feature on, then do it immediately. If it doesn't give the option of encryption, then the username and password you will enter will be insecure too. Moreover, if the camera website also doesn't have the *s* in *https*, then your feed is also not encrypted and others can easily view it.

Accessing the Camera from a Mobile Device

You also have the liberty to access the camera from your phone, but before doing that, you need to ensure that the required security feature is turned on.

Confirm that your app is up-to-date.
First, ensure that the app you are using to access the camera is up-to-date. If it is not, then update the app to the latest version.

Practice secure access.
Use a strong password and log out of the app after use. This way, no one will be able to access the app if your phone is stolen or lost.

Password-protect your phone or mobile device
Add a password to your mobile device to make it more secure.

Use a secure Wi-Fi connection.
When accessing the video feed on the phone you need to connect to a Wi-Fi. A mobile app might not provide the necessary security, but you need to ensure that you access the app on a secure network. If you access the video feed on an unsecure network then there is a fair chance that troublemakers will intercept your video feed or

they might hack your password. Thus, you should make sure that you do not access your camera's video feed through an unsecure network. You also need to make sure that your phone doesn't automatically connect to the public Wi-Fi.

Chapter 9

COOKIES: LEAVING YOUR MARK ON THE WEB

You must have noticed that the ads you see on the Internet are of your particular interest. Have you ever tried to inquire what makes it so? The answer is simple and straightforward—cookies are responsible for all this.

Now you must be wondering what a cookie is. Actually, a cookie is the information saved by the software that is used to access the Internet which is commonly known as a web browser. Cookies can be used by companies that reside in the market to collect, store, and share information about your online presence. These websites also track your behavior across the site. These cookies also help to customize your browsing experience.

G7Security.net thinks it is important to inform the users about the way the cookies are used and how they control the information about the browsing activities. The following are some answers to the common questions that people ask related to cookies.

Understanding Cookies

What Is a Cookie?
The cookie is the information that a site will save to your computer with the help of your web browser. Cookies will keep a database

of your online presence, such as a record of the pages you visit, the content you go through, and much more. This data can be used to create a profile of your online activities.

Who Places Cookies on the Web?

The first party cookies are kept on the site when you visit the site. These cookies can help improve the experience. For instance, the cookies are going to help the site remember the following things:

- The items in your shopping cart
- Your log in information
- Your preferences like the weather
- The game scores

Third-party cookies are the cookies placed by someone else on the site that you are visiting. These cookies can be by the advertising network company that is responsible for delivering the ads. For example, if you read an article about Apple products then the cookies are going to save your interest and you may see coupons for Apple products.

Controlling Cookies

How Can I Control Cookies?

There are numerous browsers available on the Internet. Different browsers allow you to delete the cookies in different ways. Before choosing the browser makes sure that the browser you choose fulfills your privacy preferences in the best possible way.

To check the setting you need to access **Settings** and then go to the **Privacy Tab** and there you will be given the option to delete the cookies or any other option related to the cookies. There are a few browsers that use add-on software to manage cookies. Security software is also responsible for managing the cookies. If you disable cookies completely, then you will limit your browsing experience. For instance, you may have to enter the information repeatedly or you may not get customized settings or ads that could prove useful to you. Some browsers help you to block third-party cookies while giving you the liberty to enable first-party cookies.

Keep Your Browser Up-to-Date

It doesn't matter which browser you are using, you need to ensure that it is updated. An old and outdated browser is going to leave your computer vulnerable to attack and you may lose important information like your log ins, passwords, or financial information. Most of the browsers update automatically, or they notify the user for the update.

What Are "Opt-Out" Cookies?

There are some websites and advertising networks that have these cookies. These cookies tell them not to use information about what sites you visit to target ads to you. There are certain ways which can help you to opt out of targeted advertising or data collection:

- You have the liberty to download add-ons to your browser that will help to control the cookies and even the opt-out cookies can be managed. Use add-ons that are trusted and have good reviews.
- The Network Advertising Initiative and the Digital Advertising Alliance are the programs from the online advertising company. They offer certain tools that will allow you to opt out of the targeted advertising.

Deleting the cookies will erase all the data downloaded on the cookies. To restore, you will have to go through the procedure all over again.

Cookies can be used for many other purposes. For instance, it can help to limit the number of times you're shown a particular ad. Thus, even if you opt out of targeted advertising, a company may still use cookies for several other purposes.

Flash Cookies

What Are Flash Cookies?
A Flash cookie is a small file that is stored on your computer by the websites that opt to use Adobe Flash Player technology. These types of cookies use the Adobe software to store the information about your online presence. These types of cookies are useful for tracking and advertising as they have the ability to store settings and preferences. When you delete cookies from your computer, you miss the Flash cookies, and they remain on your computer.

Can I Control Flash Cookies?
The latest browsers allow you the liberty to manage the Flash cookies. They give you the liberty to alter the settings through your browser settings. You might not be able to access this feature if you are using an older version. If updating the browser doesn't help then you can even look at Adobe's Website Storage Settings panel. You will be able to find the option to manage the cookies. Flash cookies are placed on your computer the next time you visit a website or view an ad unless you block Flash cookies altogether.

Private Browsing

What is "Private Browsing"?
There are several browsers that allow you to have private browsing. Private browsing settings allow you to browse the Internet without letting others know what you are doing. If your computer is being used by multiple users, then private browsing can prove to be useful because it will not retain cookies, your browsing history, search records, or the files you downloaded. It is a good habit to check your browser to see what kind of data it stores. In private browsing the cookies will not be stored after the end of the session, but the cookies used during private browsing can communicate your browsing behavior to third parties.

New Technologies

Are There Other Tracking Technologies I Should Know About?

Since there is a lot of technological advancement going on there can be some technology to track down our online presence. These are referred to as super cookies. The companies should respect your choice if they offer you opt-out options irrespective of the type of cookies used.

What Is "Do Not Track"?

Do Not Track is a tool that will allow you to hide your online presence across the web. You can turn this option on through your web browser. The web browser will send a signal to every website that you are going to visit that you do not want to be tracked down. Companies will know about your preference, and if they have committed that they will give priority to your preference, then they are bound to do so.

Chapter 10

E-COMMERCE: A FACILITY OR RISK

Compare Products Online

Are you interested in shopping online? Just spare some time to research the product as it can help save a lot of money. Despite the fact that you know what you want, if you choose from dozens of products and brand it will still be overwhelming. The following are the tips for effective shopping that will save you from scams:

Think Before You Shop
Shopping Online Infographic

Think About Your Goals Before You Shop

What kind of product do you want? What are the basic features that should be necessary in the product? What is your budget? These are the most important elements that you need to decide on before buying anything online.

Get to Know the Products in the Category

Usually the major features of a basic product and the top-of-the-line version from the same manufacturer are quite similar.

For instance, you might have to pay a few extra bucks for the toaster with a clock feature and fancy chime. You can visit the manufacturer site as it has complete information about the product features.

Use Search Engines

If you consider that you have found a good deal but the company is a bit unfamiliar, then you can search the Internet to get to know more about the company. Type in the company name along with the words *reviews, complaint,* or *scam* along with it. If you find bad reviews, that means you are investing in the wrong thing, and it is not worth the risk.

Check Comparison Shopping Sites

Comparison sites come in handy when you cannot decide between two products. These sites can also connect you to a lot of retailers who sell the same product sometimes at a different rate. Compare the total price that you will have to pay for to get the product. Your total price will include shipping, handling, and tax cost as well. Different websites have different policies thus you have to check out before the purchase whether the company will accept refunds or not. Some websites even let you get alerts of the change in price.

Consider Coupons

There are a few companies who offer discounts to the people who shop online while some of the sites list codes for free shipping and other kinds of discounts. You need to remember that coupon price does not always give the best deal. To look for the discount you can type the word *discount* or *coupon* or *free shipping* into the search bar and search for the company who offers that. You need to stay away from the websites that make you download software or access your information.

Read Reviews and Be Skeptical

When you consider a review you need to think of the source of the review. The review may come from an organization, one consumer, or from several individuals. The reviews could be fake as you may find a negative review from competitors while positive reviews from the company owners. You can look for websites that aim to present specialized and expert reviews of the products.

Evaluate What You See on Retail Sites
Scammers have different ways in which they could scam you. They set up specialty sites that sell a certain product. If you find all positive reviews on the site, then note down that there is definitely something wrong. Either the negative reviews have been deleted or the site may not include negative reviews.

What Do You Know About the Photo?
The photo of the product is going to help attract the customer this is because it should be cast in the best possible light.

What If There's a Problem?
Before the purchase you need to ask yourself a few questions like:

- What kind of reputation does the brand have?
- How long is the promised delivery time?
- What is the contact information of the seller in case of a problem?
- What are their refund policies?
- Will you be charged a restocking fee?

Shopping Online
The following are tips that are going to help with hassle-free online shopping:

Get the Details
You should know whom you are dealing with. For shopping online you could shop with almost any name. You should confirm the seller's physical address and the phone number if you have any questions regarding the seller. If you get an e-mail or a pop-up message regarding your financial information, do not reply as this is a scam and legitimate companies do not ask personal information this way.

Know What You're Buying

You should read the seller's description clearly. There may be words like *refurbished, vintage,* or *closeout* which might indicate that the product is in mint condition. Thus, you should not claim it afterward and pay accordingly.

Know What It Will Cost

Before buying you should check out the websites that offer you price comparisons. Add the shipping and the handling cost in the comparison. Avoid sending cash under any circumstances.

Check Out the Terms of the Deal

Before buying the item you need to first check out the company policies for refund and exchange. This way you will be aware of each and every policy and there will be no dispute on the shipping costs and any other costs.

Pay by Credit Card

You should pay through safer methods and paying through credit card is one of the safest ways to pay for your online shopping. The Fair Credit Billing Act is going to protect your transaction. It will also allow you the liberty to dispute charges under certain situations and you will have the option to withhold the payment while the creditor will investigate the matter. If your card is used by an unknown person then you will be responsible for a $50 charge.

Keep Records

You should keep records of your transaction that will include the product description, the price, the online receipt, and the e-mails you send and receive from the seller. Read your credit card statement so that you could report an unrecognized charge immediately.

Protect Your Information

Avoid e-mailing any financial information because this way you may be scammed. E-mail is an insecure way of transmitting information. Whenever you have to give out your financial information just make sure that the URL begins with *https*. The *s* in *https* stands for secure.

Check the Privacy Policy
It is extremely important to read the privacy policy as you should know why the company is collecting your personal information and how they are going to use it.

How to Report Online Shopping Fraud
If you are facing issues during the transaction then try to talk out the issues with the seller, buyer, or site operator. If that doesn't prove to be useful file a complaint with:

- Federal Trade Commission at www.ftc.gov/complaint
- Go to your attorney by taking contact information from at www.naag.org
- Report it to the local consumer protection agency
- Report to the Better Business Bureau

Investing Online
Investment is always a big risk, whether you are investing in your own business or not. The companies that claim they are going to be low-risk and high-reward are frauds. When you want to research about the investments you have, turn to unbiased sources such as the following:
- The U.S. Securities and Exchange Commission
- Security regulator in your state
- Securities industry self-regulatory organizations such as the Financial Industry Regulatory Authority (FINRA), Amex, and NASDAQ

It is extremely important to have an updated security software ad. You should also practice basic computer security on computers so that you could access financial accounts.

Avoid Investment Scams Online
Independently verify claims.

You should not invest in the company only because you have read an ad in the newspaper or saw a bulletin board posting specifically of the investment to be made in a small company. Companies can make huge claims about new product developments, lucrative contracts, or the company's financial health. Thus, it is recommended that you should verify these claims from the unbiased sources that are mentioned above.

Do your homework.

A lot of people get scammed because they are unaware of the frauds that are currently common in the market. When you get the offers to sell securities, you should first check whether these securities are registered or not. To check the registration check the SEC's EDGAR database and also check from the local securities regulator for more information.

Be skeptical of references.

Fraudsters are going to assure you that you are investing in a registered company. They might give you contact information so that you could verify it. When you are going to call them the attendant is going to rate the company highly. Thus, instead of reaching out to their representative, make sure to reach out to a government representative so that you are safe from the fraud they are trying to make.

Thoroughly check out promoters and company officials.

You need to thoroughly check the promoters because most fraudsters are repeat offenders. When the SEC sues them they issue a "litigation release." Thus, just run a search on litigation release for the promoter or his company to ensure that he is not a fraud or has never been involved in it before. You can also check on FINRA's free BrokerCheck service about the company and the promoter.

Find out where the stock trades are.
There are several companies on the Internet that do not meet the necessary requirements of the National Exchange Bank & Trust. Thus, the securities of these companies trade instead in the "over-the-counter" (OTC) market and they are even quoted on the OTC system. The stocks rated on OTC are the most risky ones thus avoid buying them.

Look out for high-pressure pitches.
There will be some promoters that are going to force you to invest in their offers. If this is the case, then avoid investing in such a business.

Consider the source and be skeptical.
Whenever you are offered something you should ask yourself a couple of questions such as the following:

- Why are you offered this particular tip?
- How will the promoter fit with your trade?

The one touting the stocks may be the insider of the company, or he might be paid by the company.

If you are having issues with your online investment account or you have doubts that this might be an investment scam, you should file a complaint with the SEC using the agency's Online Complaint Center. Try to include as many details as possible and write a complete summary of what happened to you. If you suspect that your personal information is being misused, then follows the steps written as follows:

- Report to the police
- Complain at the FTC website
- Visit the FTC's identity theft website for steps you can take to minimize your risk of becoming a victim

Chapter 11

KIDS AND THE TECHNOLOGY

Defend Kids Online

Kids have numerous opportunities for socializing online but there are certain risks involved in it. Parents are the ones responsible for reducing the risk of being scammed online by talking to their kids about making safe and responsible decisions.

Protecting Your Child's Privacy Online

As a parent, it is your duty to control the personal information that companies collect from your kids who are under the age of thirteen. You are empowered with tools provided by the Children's Online Privacy Protection Act. The Federal Trade Commission, the nation's consumer protection agency, enforces the COPPA Rule. The sites covered by COPPA are bound to get your consent before collecting information from your kid. They are bound to honor your choice related to the way that data will be used.

What Is COPPA?

As mentioned above, COPPA rule covers websites to protect children's personal information on websites and online services that include apps too. This rule is directed to kids under the age of thirteen. This rule is applied to general audience sites that know that they are collecting information from kids under the age of thirteen.

Now the ways in which COPPA works is that the sites that are covered by COPPA are bound to get permission directly from the parents if they intend to collect, use, or disclose their child's information. Personal information detailing the world of COPPA include the name of the kid, his address, phone number or e-mail address as well as the physical locations, photos, videos, and audio recordings of the kid. Under the act of COPPA personal identifiers like IP addresses, which can be used to access the location of the kid, are also protected.

Does COPPA Affect the Sites and Services My Kids Use?

If the website doesn't take information from your kid then COPPA is nowhere. COPPA comes into action only when particular personal information is taken from your kid. Actually, COPPA makes you responsible for your child's personal information.

How Does COPPA Work?

Now we are going to discuss the way COPPA works. For instance, a child wants to use some features for which he has to sign up and provide personal details. Before registering you should get a plain language notice about the details that they are going to collect from your kid and the way in which they are going to use that information. Parents have to provide their consent for gathering their kid's personal information. The sites will notify you of the place where you could provide the consent.

The notice will have a link to the privacy policy. That privacy policy will be plain and easy to read. It will be in a language that will be easy to understand for you. The privacy policy should mention the details of the information that it will collect and the way it will be used. For instance, if the company plans to sell your kid's information than the privacy statement should also mention the details of the company to whom the information will be sold. It should also include contact information on whom you can contact and someone will answer your question.

The notice should also include the details that will tell the parents the way to give their consent. Different sites and services have different ways, some may ask you to send a permission slip or some may ask you to contact the office.

What Are the Choices Given to the Parents?

The first and foremost choice that is given to the parents is whether they are comfortable with the information provided by the site.

The second is the most important choice and that depends upon your consent. In this choice you will let the company know how much consent you will give to the company.

Once you have given the permission to collect the personal information that doesn't mean that you have lost control over the information. You are still the boss. You can review the information and you still have the right to get that information deleted. As you are the parent you have the right to retract the consent and make sure that the given information is properly deleted.

What to Do If It Looks Like the Site Is Breaking the Rules?

There are certain websites that do so but it is quite rare to find such a case because parents have the right to report the website. If you think that the site that collected your child's information is marketing the information in the wrong way or it violates any of the conditions stated in the privacy policy then you may report it to the FTC at FTC. Gov/complaint.

Child Identity Theft

Your child's information is extremely important to you. Suppose your child's information gets stolen by a scammer and he uses it to get a job, government benefits, medical care, utilities, or a car loan. He can even get a mortgage by using the information. You can do a lot to protect your child's personal information and to reduce the damage that is caused by child identity theft.

Warning Signs

You will get several warning signs that can tip you off to the fact that someone is misusing your kid's information. For instance,

- Your child gets bills or notices for products or services you haven't utilized. These bills may also include medical services used.
- Your kid is turned down from a government benefit and presented with the reason that he is already being paid in another account through a Social Security number.
- You get a notice that your kid hasn't paid taxes on income or any other issue related to it.

Check for a Credit Report

If you have doubts that your child's identity is being stolen, then the first thing you need to do is to check his credit card report. You can contact nationwide credit reporting companies that are written as follows:

- Equifax: 1-800-525-6285
- Experian: 1-888-397-3742
- TransUnion: childidtheft@transunion.com

You need to ask them to search with the help of your child's name and SSN. If you are unable to locate the issue, then ask for a so-called manual search.

If your child has a credit report, you need to follow up with each and every credit-reporting company. First of all, you will be bound to prove that your child is a minor and you are the parent or the legal guardian. Ask all the companies to remove all the accounts, account inquiries, and collection notices from any file associated with your child's name and Social Security number.

Repair the Damage

If you suspect that your child's identity is being misused, then you should inform one of the following credit-reporting companies:

- Equifax: 1-800-525-6285
- Experian: 1-888-397-3742
- TransUnion: 1-800-680-7289

The company you will report to will issue an alert to all three companies, along with any of the reports that are associated with your child's name or SSN. These alerts will be in action for ninety days.

You can also file a report with the FTC by visiting their site at FTC. Gov/complaint or by calling them at 1-877-438-4338. You might also have to file a police report because of the medical services or the taxes. In the end, contact all the companies where your information was misused and request them to close the fraudulent account and mark it to show that it was a case of child identity theft. If you need more details on this topic you might be interested to see Safeguarding Your Child's Future.

Prevention equals Protection

You can take up some necessary steps to protect your child's identity:

- Make sure that you have kept all the necessary documents of your child's identity locked up.
- Avoid sharing the child's SSN with unknown companies and parties. If you really trust the other party and share the number, then ensure that it will be protected by going through the privacy rules. Or you may try to use any other identifier.
- Make sure that you shred all documents that show your child's personal information if you want to throw it away.

- You need to be proactive in certain circumstances, such as when a kid is being adopted; your wallet, which had your kid's SSN, is stolen; or any other such event that might threaten the identity of your kid.

When Your Child Turns Sixteen

Responsible parents usually check their kid's credit report before their sixteenth birthday. You need to go through it to check for fraud or misuse so that you have time to correct it before the kid applies for a job, a loan, or an apartment.

Kids and Mobile Phones

Mobile phones have become a necessity in this modern age. But have you ever wondered what age is appropriate for a kid to have a mobile phone? That is a decision that parents need to take as parents best understand their kids. You need to consider your child's age, personality, maturity, and your family's circumstances. When you think it is the right time to hand over a phone to your kid then teach them about safety and responsibility.

Phones, Features, and Options

Make a decision on options and features for your kid's phone.
When buying a mobile phone for your kid you should make sure that you have some choices for privacy settings of your phone and child safety controls. There are several such carriers who allow parents to manage and control the features like web access, texting, or downloading. Some cell phones are specially made for kids. They are easy to use and have limited features with exclusive emergency buttons.

Make smart moves with your kid's smartphones.
There are several such mobile phones that offer web access and mobile apps. But, if you are concerned with the content that your kid might view online, you can choose web filtering or buy a phone with limited Internet access.

Get your hands on social mapping.
There are several mobile phones that have GPS technology embedded on them. This way kids can get to know about their friends and their friends can get to know about them. You need to educate your kids that they should use this kind of feature only with the ones they trust and not broadcast their location 24/7. Parents can also use this service to know about the location of their kid.

Develop Cell Phone Rules
Elaborate what you expect from kids after giving them the phone.
You need to talk to the kids to let them know where it is appropriate to use their phones. You would also want to establish rules for using these products responsibly. Tell them that they are not allowed to use cell phones during family time or any other time you want.

Do not give leverage to kids to involve in bullying.
Kids can use their phones to bully other kids. Educate your kids that these things do matter a lot and there is no replacement for manners and ethics. Ask them to treat other kids the same way they want to be treated.

Set an example.
You are the one whom your kid is going to follow. If you are using the phone at the dinner table then your kid will also use it. Just make sure you practice what you say so that you could set an example for your kids.

Mobile sharing and networking.
Mobile sharing and network will present unique opportunities but also challenges too. Although these things can foster creativity and fun they also bring in problems related to personal reputation and safety.

Be careful when sharing photos and videos.

The latest phones have a camera and video capability, and this makes it easy for teens to capture and share each and every moment. Educate your teens to make them realize that they need to be careful about the things they share via cell phone as it could be embarrassing, and it could even be unsafe. It becomes a lot more difficult to control the damage caused after photos have been shared.

Try using respectable decisions with mobile social networking.

There are several social networking sites that have a feature that will allow the user to check their profiles and post comments on the different things that they have shared. Filters won't help in this situation but if you talk to your kids in this aspect then it might help.

Kids and Socializing Online

Socializing online is a common practice nowadays as there are numerous social networking websites available online. But it is extremely important to inform your kid that they need to navigate these spaces carefully. The trend of socializing has brought in the options of sharing too much information and posting comments, photos, or videos that may result in damaging someone's feelings and reputation. The following are some ways in which these pitfalls could be reduced:

- Judging the situation as you do in the real world might help a lot in reducing the risk.
- Your kids should be aware of the fact that every action has a reaction.
- Tell them that what they post or say online may have consequences offline.

Educate Kids to Post Only What They are Comfortable with Others Seeing

Your child's posts might be seen by a broader audience thus you must ensure that they post the right things on their walls even if the privacy settings are high. You need to encourage your child to think about the language they use online and to think before posting pictures and videos.

Remind the Kids That Action Cannot Be Taken Back

Your kids should know that even if they delete the inappropriate information afterward, they will have little control over the older versions that exist on other people's computers. It may even circulate all around the Internet.

Impersonating Is a Crime

You need to let your kids know that it is not right to create sites, pages, or posts that impersonate other people, like their teacher, friend, and so forth.

Inform Your Kids to Limit What They Share

You should help your kids understand the fact that there is some information that needs to stay private. You should tell your kids that it is extremely vital to keep some information hidden. You can even tell them the results of leaking personal information.

Educate Your Kids to Avoid Sex Talk Online

Research proves that the teenagers who do not talk about sex with strangers are not much likely to come in contact with predators. When teens are contacted by adults, they find it creepy. If something like this happens, then let them know that they must block these people without hesitating.

Make Your Kids Learn Online Manners

Do not shout at your kids as they might try to run away from you. Talk to your kids with politeness and tell them to be courteous online as well.

Tone It Down

Make your kids learn that people usually understand well when they are told anything in a polite way. Thus, they should also tone their way of communication in a polite way.

Cc: and Reply All: with Care

You need to suggest to your kids to resist sending messages to everyone stored in their contact list.

Alter Settings to Limit Access to Your Profile

Use privacy settings.

There are several social networking websites that allow the user to alter their privacy settings. This way you can resist against the ones who could view your profile. Educate your kids about the importance of these settings and tell them that you expect to be allowed to view their profile.

Parents should ensure that the security settings on the chat and video accounts should be high. There exist such chat programs that give leverage to the parents to control whether people in the contact list of their kid can view their status when they are online. Parents can also determine who can send messages to their kids or they may block anyone on the list.

Use a safe screen name.

You can encourage your kids to think about the impression that impressive screen names could make. A good screen name will hide a lot of information. This information will hide the age of your kids, their location, or their gender. Tell the kids not to use the names that are being used in their e-mail addresses.

Review your child's friend list.

You would definitely want to keep a check on your kid's friend list. It is extremely important to do so because you will not want to have a wrong person in your kid's contact list.

Get to Know About Your Kids' Online Activities
Keep an eye on your kids' online activity.
You should know what social networking websites your kids are visiting so that you could keep an eye on them. If you are concerned about the online behavior of your kids then try to search the websites they use to see the information they post.

Talk to your kids about their online activity.
Talk to your kids to get to know who they are talking to when their friends are offline.

Embolden your kids to have faith in their gut.
Tell your kids that if they feel threatened by someone or they are uncomfortable because of anything they see online, then they should trust their gut and take the necessary actions. You can even help them report their concerns to the police department and the management of the site.

Kids and Computer Security
You should be fully aware of the fact that the security of your computer will also affect the safety of your kid's online experience and even your experience too. Thus, it is important to talk to your kids about computer security and tell them the ways to protect your computer.

Teaching Computer Security
You need to educate your kids about computer security.

- Tell them that information like their Social Security numbers, account numbers, and passwords should be kept private.
- Tell them that, if they are being offered something, to be careful about it because there might be malware hiding in it. Just check that product with the security software and then use it.

- Tell them the importance of using strong passwords and the ways to protect them. Long passwords are difficult to crack; thus it is important to tell them to use strong passwords.

You should also make sure that your family computers are protected by suitable security software.

P2P File Sharing

Some kids love to share music, games, and software online, but they do not realize the risk involved in it. These things are shared through peer-to-peer file sharing which allow people to share files through an informal network of computers running a single kind of software. Some of the most common risks involved in files shared through P2P are:

- People may provide access to the to their private files accidently.
- If you download copyrighted material then you may get into legal issues.
- A shared file could be a malware, spyware, or pornography.

Let your kids know the following tips so that they can surf the Internet safely:

- Ensure that you install file-sharing software properly. Make sure that the software has the proper settings so that private information is safe from being accessed.
- Before using any downloaded file, your kids should make sure that they properly scanned it through updated security software.

Phishing

Phishing is a process in which you receive a fake text, e-mail, or pop-up message so that people share their personal and financial information with others. The information shared will be used to commit identity theft.

The following are some of the most common tips and tricks that can help kids avoid phishing:

- Tell your kids not to reply to the text, e-mail, or pop-up message that asks for personal information and do not follow the links given in them.
- Educate your kids about the attachments that come with e-mails. Be cautious about opening any attachment or downloading any files from e-mails you receive regardless of who sent them. Unexpected files may contain malware.

You need to get your kids involved so that they can develop careful Internet habits. It would be a good option to show your kids the phishing message you get as they will learn quickly that way.

Apps
The phones of the modern world allow you the opportunity to download apps. These apps use your personal information as well. Thus, it is important to read the privacy policy and get to know how they are going to use the information they are taking from you. Suggest to your kids that they read the privacy policy of each and every app they use.

Kids and Virtual Worlds
The first thing that pops in our minds is "what is a virtual world?" Actually, a virtual world is the computer-simulated online places where people use different characters to represent themselves. These characters could be avatars, graphic characters, or cartoon characters. There are several such sites that claim that they are for kids but, by adding up the age limit feature, cannot stop teens from using them.

Types of Virtual Worlds
There are some virtual worlds that are specially made for young kids and teenagers. There are certain built-in protections that will help to keep their exercises age-appropriate while others

are designed especially for adults. These virtual worlds can be accessed in several different ways. Some can be accessed through a multiplayer game with help of a gaming console while others are accessed through online communities where avatars' activities rely on their users' imaginations.

Educate Your Kids to Your Kids
Kids find a way to get into these virtual spaces one way or the other. Thus, restriction to Internet access or smartphone access is not a solution to the problem of accessing inappropriate content. You need to educate them by talking to them about this issue in detail. You need to make them understand that personal information about them, their family members, and friends should stay private. You can even talk to them about avoiding sex talk or sexual situations online.

Stay Engaged
If your child is using a virtual world, then keep an eye on him. Get to know the site he is visiting and the privacy details. Ensure that it verifies age in an appropriate manner.

If your child's behavior is changing and he is excessively involved in the activities that are offered in virtual worlds, then you should have a check on the sites he is visiting. No one else knows your kid better than you do, so you need to make sure of the sites that are best for your kid.

Chapter 12

THE BASICS OF CLOUD COMPUTING

What is the cloud?

Cloud computing is a term that is getting a lot of attention these days. You can find numerous articles in publication and even among users. You will now find individuals frequently talking about the technology.

Cloud computing is a type of computing in which you subscribe to the services available online. This particular style of computing is based on the shared, elastic resources delivered to users in a self-service, metered manner using web technologies. This is the actual definition of cloud computing, but when you go out and ask people what cloud computing basically is, you will get different answers from everyone. This is because cloud computing is serving them in different ways, and they are going to define it in the way it is serving them.

If you want to fully understand the benefits of cloud computing across the enterprise, then first you need to understand the functional benefits that it is providing its customers. There are different people in organizations that get benefits from this service. Cloud computing benefits different roles in different ways. Here, in this article, we are going to discuss the ways in which these different roles get the advantage from this particular technology.

Let's assume you are on a trip or at work and you have to access your e-mail, then cloud computing will present you the best solution in this situation. Your e-mail is quite different from the software installed on your computer. Word processing is a type of software that stores the files on your computer. Now if you want to access that particular document on the go, then cloud computing is going to provide you the opportunity to access these documents on the go.

How can you use the cloud?

Cloud computing is going to allow you the opportunity to access the documents on the go. In traditional computing ways, you have to bring the device along with you so that you could access the files stored on it. But since the introduction of cloud computing, the need to carry along the device has vanished. The cloud provider is going to host both the software and the hardware within itself to provide you with the services at home or in business.

Cloud computing has made life easier for, not only the business men, but also for the individuals. Talking from a professional's aspect. it is highly significant to travel along with important information but in a secure way. This is the reason why cloud computing is rated as an extremely significant invention of the modern world. The following are some other reasons that have improved its value in the market:

- Easy to maintain and manage
- The company has to pay only for the services it is using
- The company is not responsible for upgrading
- The company can use as much as it needs and then it can pay for what it has used
- Ease of accessing personal documents from anywhere just by legally passing through the security check.

One of the most essential requirements that you need to fulfill is that you need to have a strong Internet connection so that you could access the cloud services without any hassle.

This means that if you want to access something from the cloud, you need to have an Internet connection. This Internet connection could be wired, wireless, or through a mobile connection. The major benefit that you get from it is that you could access things on the go.

Types of cloud computing

There are different types of clouds that are available in the market. You can access these services according to your demand. Public cloud services prove to be most useful for private users and small businesses.

Public Cloud: It is a cloud service that could be accessed by anyone who has an Internet connection and a cloud service subscription.

Private Cloud: Private cloud has been established just for a limited group or an organization. Not everyone has access to the cloud service.

Community Cloud: In community cloud, two or more organizations share a single cloud that has similar requirements.

Hybrid Cloud: This is the combination of at least two clouds which are a mixture of public, private, or community clouds.

Choosing a cloud provider

Cloud services have become a lot more common in this modern world; thus the people who provide these services have also increased, and there is tough competition out there in the market. The services provided by the providers vary from company to company. But when you choose a provider, you need to ensure that they fulfill your needs. Your needs are going to vary according to your use. For instance, if you will need cloud services for your home, then your requirements will be different while, if you need it for your business, then your requirements will be different. The only aspect you need to keep in mind is that these clouds are going to provide services as you go.

There are three major types of services available in the market, which are defined as follows. These three services differ in the amount of control that they provide to the user.

- Software as a Service
  This service is also commonly known as SaaS. In this type of service, the service provider offers access to both resources and the applications. When you are using SaaS services, then you do not require a physical copy of the software in your device. It also makes it possible for you to access the software on all the devices at once just by accessing the cloud. In this service, you have less control over the cloud.

- Platform as a Service
  PaaS is a common name for this service. This is a better service than SaaS. In this type of service, the users are provided with the components that they need to develop and operate applications.

- Infrastructure as a Service
  With this type of service, the whole infrastructure is provided as a service. The user is not bound to buy any resources stored in this service and only pays for what he uses.

As the list grows, the control over the cloud increases. The cloud provider has less control in an IaaS service as compared to SaaS service.

So what should home users or businesses that are looking to start assess from it? They need to assess the level of control they will be provided over for their information and the types of services that they desire to have from a cloud provider. For instance, you are starting off your business and you cannot afford the computing infrastructure. In this situation, IaaS is the best solution to this problem as it will charge you as much as you use and will not require any huge investment.

But you might have to spend more money on the resources, on the development, and on the operation of applications. So before subscribing to a cloud service, you need to make sure that you evaluate your current computational resources and the standard of control that you desire to have, the financial position you have, and if you see a future in the business.

If you are a home user, you will definitely be looking for a cloud service that is less costly and gives you a lower level of control. You will not be bothered about the numerous other complex cloud offerings. Thus, it is extremely important to clarify your requirements so that you can easily decide ahead on which kind of service you will require. After you have done this, research on the cloud providers. Go online to read reviews about them and research on their history. This way, you will be able to get a better idea of what is right for you and what is going to suit you the best.

Security
You cannot remove the element of insecurity in the cloud as well. The people coming in with malicious intent will consider the information as quite valuable. People store quite useful and potentially secure information in their computer, but now this information is being transferred into the cloud. The security measures that the cloud provider takes are critical for you to understand, but it is extremely important for you to take proper security measures so that your data is safe from going into the wrong hands.

The first and the foremost aspect that you need to look into is what kind of security measure your cloud provider already has in place. These security measures are different for every service provider. You need to check upon the following aspects:

- What is the method of encryption being used?
- What are the methods of protection being used for actual hardware that your data will be stored in?
- Does the company maintain backups of your data?
- Does the company maintain firewalls?
- If the company is using community cloud, then what are the precautions they are taking to protect the information from other companies?

Most of the cloud service providers have standard terms and conditions that may answer all your questions, but the home user will have little chance to negotiate with the cloud service provider, whereas a small-business owner might have a little room to discuss the terms of their contract with the service provider. Thus, he will get the chance to ask these questions from him. You can ask several other questions as well, but the major concern for both of you should be the security of your data.

When you shift to cloud services, you shift the control to an external source irrespective of the fact that you are overly careful about the data. The distance between you and the physical location of the data creates a barrier between the both of you.

Thus, it may also create space for a third party to access your personal information. So it is important that you give up direct control of your data so that you could utilize the full benefits of using the cloud. On the contrary, you need to keep in mind that there are several such cloud providers that have a huge knowledge of the ways to keep your data safe. A provider will have more resources and the expertise to keep your network, data, and computers more secure than a normal user.

To summarize what is being said above, the cloud provides many facilities not only to the home users but also in the businesses. It has opened a completely diverse world of computing. It has shown the broad range of uses and increases the ease of use by giving access through Internet connection. But with ease comes drawbacks. You have a lot less control over your information as compared to the times when you had all the data in your computer. You might not know exactly where your data is stored. Cloud technology is a big target for hackers, and it is quite vulnerable to attacks because cloud networks can be accessed through an unsecured Internet connection.

If you are thinking of using the cloud, then be sure about what information you should keep in it, who will have access to that information, and what are the basic things that you will require to make sure that it is well protected in the cloud. Moreover, you need to be sure about what your needs are and what kind of provider is going to suit you best.

Chapter 13

Technology and the Associated Risks

This section is going to provide an introduction to the technologies that lie beneath the Internet. The details of the technologies are written with an aspect of a novice end user. Subsections are going to provide a short overview of the topic.

A. What Does Broadband Mean?

Broadband is a term that is used to point out high-speed network connections. Internet connections that are connected via a cable modem and digital subscriber line (DSL) are known as broadband Internet connections. Basically, *bandwidth* is a term that is used to describe the relative speed of a network connection. For instance, dial-up connections support an Internet connection of 56 Kbps. Although there is no threshold required for a connection that could be referred as broadband, the most common speed that you will find in broadband connections is 1 Mbps.

B. What Is Cable Modem Access?

Cable modem allows only one computer to connect to the Internet. It connects the computer to the network through a cable TV network. The cable modem has an Ethernet LAN connection to the computer, and it can reach a speed of 5 Mbps.

Typically, the speeds are lower than the maximum speed told above, but since the cable providers turn the whole neighborhood into LAN, thus they share the same bandwidth. Due to this shared medium topology, cable modem users experience slow network access during the peak hours. In addition to that, these networks will also be a lot more vulnerable to attacks.

C. What Is DSL Access?
DSL is the common name of digital subscriber line. It provides users with a dedicated bandwidth. But the maximum bandwidth available to a single user is lower than the bandwidth allowed in cable modem because of the differences in the network technologies. Dedicated bandwidth is only dedicated between your home and the DSL provider's central office. There is no guarantee of the bandwidth all the way across the Internet. DSL network is not vulnerable to packet sniffing, but there are several other security risks attached with it.

D. How Are Broadband Services Different from Traditional Dial-up Services?
The dial-up services are known as dial-up demand services. Thus, it means that your computer connects to the Internet only when it demands network access such as e-mail or a request to load a web page. When there is no more data to send, or after a certain amount of idle time, the computer disconnects the call. In each case, a call connects to a pool of modems at the ISP. Every time you connect, you are assigned a different IP address. Thus, it becomes a lot more difficult for an attacker to take advantage of vulnerable network services so that it can take control of your computer.

Broadband services are the services that are always on because in broadband services, you do not need to call in order to set up a connection when your computer has to send something. The computer is always on the network ready to send or receive data through the network interface card (NIC). Since it will be always connected, your computer's IP address will not change frequently—thus making it more vulnerable to attack.

Several broadband service providers use well-known IP addresses for the home users. So there might be a possibility that an attacker might not be able to single out your specific computer as yours. But these attackers will know that your service provider's broadband customers are within a certain address range. This way, your computer will become a lot more vulnerable to the attack than it was before.

The table given below will show a brief comparison between the broadband services and the dial-up services that were used before.

Table 2: Comparison of Dial-up and Broadband Services

	Dial-up	**Broadband**
Connection type	Dial on demand	Always on
IP address	Changes on each call	Static or infrequently changing
Relative connection speed	Low	High
Remote control potential	The computer must be dialed in to control remotely	The computer is always connected so remote control can occur anytime
ISP-provided security	Little or none	Little or none

E. How Is Broadband Access Different from the Network I Use at Work?

Confidential programs and the files in corporate and government networks are usually protected by several layers of security that may range from network firewall to encryption. They also hire support staff to maintain the availability of these networks.

You are responsible for your own computer. You will definitely not have a staff to manage and operate your home network; thus your computer will be a lot more vulnerable to these attacks. Thus, you need to take certain precautions so that you are able to save your device from the attacks.

F. What Is a Protocol?
Protocol is the well-defined rules and regulations that will allow computers to communicate over a network. You can even say that protocol acts the same way as grammar acts in a language.

G. What Is IP?
IP stands for Internet protocol. As mentioned above, protocol is the set of rules that allow communication over a network—thus, in the same way, that is how Internet protocol works. IP contains a set of rules that allow devices to communicate over the Internet. There are a lot more definitions given on the Internet and other places, but we are going to mention just a little in detail. We are going to discuss other terms related to it such as IP addresses, static vs. dynamic addressing, NAT, and TCP and UDP Ports.

If you want to have an overview of TCP/IP, then you can visit the following links to get to know about them:

* http://www.faqs.org/faqs/internet/tcp-ip/tcp-ip-faq/part1/
* http://www.faqs.org/faqs/internet/tcp-ip/tcp-ip-faq/part2/

H. What Is an IP Address?
IP addresses are similar to phone numbers. When you have to call someone, you need to know their telephone number. Similarly, when one computer needs to connect to the other, it must first know its IP address. IP addresses are usually shown as 192.168.62.231.

When you are unaware of the telephone number, then you try to locate the number in a diary. But in the case of IP addresses, the directory is known as *domain name system*, or DNS for short. When you are going to write www.cert.org in the search bar, the computer is going to go and ask the DNS to locate the numeric IP address associated with it.

Each and every computer on the Internet is associated with an IP address. The major aim of the IP address is to uniquely identify the computer. But the address may change when,

- the computer is dialing into an Internet Service Provider (ISP),
- the computer is connected behind the firewall,
- or the computer is connected to a broadband service, and it uses the dynamic IP addressing.

I. What Is Static and Dynamic Addressing?
We can get a static IP address when an ISP permanently assigns one or more IP address for each and every user. Static IP addresses do not change frequently; but if a static address is assigned and not used, then it is wasted. Since there is a limited number of an IP address available, it is important to allocate them in a smart way.

Dynamic IP addresses are completely different from static ones. These addresses could change over time. These IP addresses allow the ISP to efficiently utilize their address space. If a dynamic IP address is not being used, then it is given to some other device instead of being wasted.

J. What Is NAT?
NAT is the abbreviation of *network address translation*. It provides a way to hide the IP addresses. These are usually used to hide a private network from the Internet. The computer is still able to access the Internet. NAT is used in many ways, but the most common use of it is "masquerading" that is used by home users. Most of the firewall support NAT masquerading. Using this particular method, one or more devices on the LAN can be made

to appear as a single IP address to the outside Internet. This way, all the computers in a home network will use a single cable modem or DSL connection without needing an ISP to provide more than one IP address.

K. What Are TCP and UDP ports?
TCP is a transmission control protocol, and UDP stands for user datagram protocol. These are both protocols that use IP. These two protocols are responsible for the applications, which are also known as services, to talk to each other.

For instance, a different telephone number and a mailbox number may be assigned to more than one person; similarly, the computer might have several applications such as word processing or e-mail applications that run on the same IP address. Ports allow them to differentiate the services. Port is a number that is associated with each application. The duty of the port is to uniquely identify the service that application will give to that computer. Some common port numbers are 80 for web (HTTP), 25 for e-mail (SMTP), and 53 for domain name system (DNS).

L. What Is a Firewall?
A firewall is basically the system or group of systems that forces an access control policy between two networks. In home networks, there are two forms of firewalls, which are mentioned below:

- Software firewall—a special software running on the computer.
- Network firewall—a device designed to protect more than one computer. It is dedicated to that particular network.

Both are a type of firewall that come with one sole purpose, and that is to define access policies for inbound connections to the computers they are protecting. There are several others that provide the ability to control what kind of services (ports) the protected computers are able to use to access the Internet. For home users,

121

firewalls come with preconfigured security policies from which the user is given the choice to choose while some are designed in a way that they can be configured according to the need.

M. What Does Antivirus Software Do?

There are countless antivirus software programs available in the market. All these software programs operate differently. They behave in the way the vendor chooses them to behave. The only thing that is common among all these antivirus programs is that they all look for the pattern in the files or the memory of the computer that shows that there is the presence of malware in your computer.

You need to update the antivirus software as soon as the new update comes on the market because new viruses are discovered daily. The antivirus is effective only when it has the latest virus profiles installed on your computer so that it can look for recently discovered viruses. Thus, it is important to keep the profiles up-to-date.

Computer security risks to home users

A. What Is at Risk?

There are three major concerns of information security. They are as follows:

- Confidentiality—information should only be available to those who have legal right to access it.
- Integrity—only those who have legal access should be allowed to modify it.
- Availability—the information should be accessible to those who legally require it.

These concepts apply to both home users and Internet users. You will definitely not want a stranger to look through your documents. Similarly, you will want to keep the tasks confidential. Your tasks may include e-mails to friends and family, other financial transactions, or any other task. You also need to ensure that the information you enter should remain intact and it is available when you need it.

Some of the security risks start from the likelihood of international misuse of the data by intruders through the Internet. Even if you are not connected to the Internet, the risk of losing data isn't completely nullified. For instance, there are some natural factors like hard disk failures, theft, and power outages that may also result in loss of data. Although you cannot avoid the possibility of the risk, you are definitely able to take certain steps that would allow you to reduce the effort of recovering from the loss. Before pointing out the ways in which you could protect your computer or home network, we are going to look at some of the most common risks.

B. Intentional Misuse of Your Computer
The most common techniques used by hackers and the intruders that allow them to gain control of your home computer are listed below:

- Trojan horse programs
- Backdoor and remote administration programs
- Denial of service
- Being a midway for another attack
- Unprotected Windows shares
- Mobile code (Java, JavaScript, and ActiveX)
- Cross-site scripting
- E-mail spoofing
- E-mail-borne viruses
- Hidden file extensions
- Chat clients
- Packet sniffing

Trojan Horse Programs
Trojan horse programs are one of the most common ways for the intruders trick you. This particular program is also known as social engineering. They install backdoor programs to get access to your computer. This way, they get easy access without letting the owner know about it.

Backdoor and Remote Administration Programs
The computers that have Windows operating system installed on them can be accessed by the intruders if they have BackOrifice, Netbus, and SubSeven installed on them. These programs, once installed, will allow remote access to other's computers.

Denial of Service
There is one other form of attack that is known as the denial-of-service attack. This type of attack causes your computer to crash, or it becomes busy processing data and you are unable to use it. In most of the cases, the latest antivirus patches will prevent the attack. It is possible that your computer is used as a participant in a denial-of-service attack on other systems, and you could also be a target of this particular attack.

Being an Intermediary for Another Attack
If your computer is attacked, your device may be used for launching attacks on other systems. A common example of this is the way distributed denial-of-service (DDoS) tools are used. Intruders install an agent that is also known as a Trojan horse program into your computer, which waits for further instructions. A single handler is enough to instruct a number of agents to launch a denial-of-service attack on another system. Thus, the end target is not your computer, but it is someone else's computer.

Unprotected Windows Shares
The people who use unprotected Windows shared are easily exploited by intruders in an automated way. They can easily place tools on a large number of Windows-based computers that are

attached to the Internet. Since the site security is interdependent on the Internet, a vulnerable computer is not only a big problem for the owner but also for the other sites too. The risk increases as the number of computers connected to the Internet increases. The risk is doubled if these computers connect to the Internet with unprotected Windows. These risks are described in detail in the following link: http://www.cert.org/incident_notes/IN-2000-01. html.

The other threat that the computer systems of the modern world face is the threat of malicious and destructive code, such as viruses or worms. These programs leverage the unprotected Windows networking shares to propagate. An example of 911 worms is described in the link below:
http://www.cert.org/incident_notes/IN-2000-03.html.

Mobile Code (Java, JavaScript, and ActiveX)
Mobile code has also shown lots of problems. For instance, people have reported problems with Java, JavaScript, and ActiveX. These are the programming languages that allow the developers to write the code that could be run on your browser. The code is useful, but it can be used by the intruders to gain access to the information. The users have the option to disable the Java, JavaScript, and ActiveX in your web browser. You need to disable them just to protect your computer from that risk.

Cross-Site Scripting
If you are visiting a malicious website, then the web developer will attach a script that will be transferred to your web browser. The developer is going to send a form or a database inquiry in which the malicious script will be hidden. The following things are going to expose your web browser to malicious scripts:

- Clicking the links on the web pages, e-mail messages, or newsgroup postings without having an idea where these links are going to take you.

- Using interactive websites on an unknown website.
- Viewing online discussion groups, forums, or other dynamically generated pages. These users will allow the users to post text containing HTML tags.

E-mail Spoofing

E-mail spoofing is a way to trick the user who receives the e-mail. The user who receives the message thinks that he received it from some other source, which is a reliable one—thus he clicks on it. This way, the malicious content gets into the computer, and your computer will become an agent to the handlers.

Spoofed e-mails can be harmless pranks while some can do it as a social ploy. Examples are written as follows:

- E-mails that are sent from the administrators and request you to change your password to specific strings. They even threaten you that if you do not do so, your account will be suspended.
- E-mail from a person in authority asking you to send a copy of private information.

Your service providers may request you to change your passwords but they will not request you to change it to a specified string or a number. Moreover, companies do not ask for you to share your personal documents via e-mail. If you have a doubt that someone has sent you a spoof e-mail then you may report it to the service provider.

E-mail-borne Viruses

You may even get malicious code as an attachment, so you need to be careful before opening the attachments that come in e-mails. You need to be sure about the source of the e-mail so that you do not download spam into your computer. The Melissa virus was a virus that spread because it originated from a familiar address. Nowadays, many viruses take social engineering to spread.

You should never run a program unless or until you are sure about the fact that it is authored by a person or a company that you trust. You should also avoid sending programs that do not have legal owners to your friends and family because they might contain a virus.

Hidden File Extensions

Windows operating system has a vulnerability—it has the option to hide the file extension for known file types turned on by default. The user has the opportunity to disable these features so that file extensions are displayed by Windows. E-mail-borne viruses are blamed to exploit this particular extension. The VBS/Love Letter worm was the first virus that took advantage of this vulnerability. It, by the name of *LOVE-LETTER-FOR-YOU.TXT.vbs*, was sent through an e-mail. Some of the other malicious programs have incorporated similar naming schemes. Examples include the following:

- Downloader (MySis.avi.exe or QuickFlick.mpg.exe)
- VBS/Timofonica (TIMOFONICA.TXT.vbs)
- VBS/CoolNote (COOL_NOTEPAD_DEMO.TXT.vbs)
- VBS/OnTheFly (AnnaKournikova.jpg.vbs)

The files sent through them seem to be harmless with known extensions. Other file types that are sent through e-mail are .vbs or .exe that helps to add spam into the computer.

Chat Clients

Instant messaging and Internet relay chat are currently two of the most famous chatting applications in the Internet world. They provide a mechanism in which the information can be transmitted in a bidirectional way between the Internet and the computers. Chat clients will provide people who could send messages, share URLs, and, in many cases, files as well. Since chat clients allow executable code, the risk of attacks is kind of similar to those of e-mail clients. In chatting applications, you need to be careful while downloading files. In addition to that, you need to be careful about exchanging files with unknown parties.

Packet Sniffing

Packet sniffer is a program that catches data from the packet that travels over the Internet. The data might include personal information such as passwords, usernames, and other important financial information. Intruders catch passwords through packet sniffers and then crack into your account to either steal or to use your computer to launch attacks on others. You will not require admin level access if you want to install a packet sniffer.

Cable modem and dial-up users are more vulnerable to packet sniffing because entire neighborhoods of cable modem are effectively part of the same LAN. This makes the computers connected to this network more vulnerable to the attack of packet sniffing. If a packet sniffer is installed on any cable modem user's computer in a neighborhood, then there is a fair chance that it can capture data transmitted by any other cable modem in the same neighborhood.

C. Accidents and Other Risks

There are several other risks that your computer faces in terms of physical accidents. These types of risks do not involve an Internet connection. Most of these risks are well known; thus we do not go into a lot of detail in this book. Most of the practices that are related to these risks may also help to condense defenselessness to the network-based risks discussed above.

Disk Failure

Disk failures are one of the most common issues that computers face these days. There is always a chance of disk failure when we talk about things of a mechanical nature. You cannot remove the chance of hardware crash because mechanical devices are always vulnerable to these kinds of things. The only way to avoid losing data through it is by regularly backing up data.

Power Failure and Surges

Power problems such as surges, blackouts, and brownouts can physically damage your computer. Power problems are going to induce a hard disk crash, or it will damage other components of the computer. Thus, you need to use uninterrupted power supplies or other such things that are going to help you save your computer from damage.

Physical Theft

Theft is one act that can happen to anyone. If your laptop is going to be stolen, then you are definitely going to lose your data. To avoid these things, you need to have regular backups of your data so that if, unfortunately, such an event happens to you, your data will not be lost. Cryptographic tools are available that can encrypt the data stored on the computer. CERT/CC recommends the use of these tools because your computer might contain sensitive data.

Actions home users can take to protect their computer systems

The following are some of the activities that CERT/CC recommends to home users:

- If you work from home, you need to consult the system support individual.
- Try using an antivirus software to protect your computers.
- Protect your computer with a firewall.
- Don't try to open unknown e-mails.
- Avoid running programs that have unknown extensions.
- Avoid running programs of unknown origin.
- Disable the option of hidden filename extensions.
- Patch all the applications, even your operating system.
- Disconnect from the network.
- Try to disable Java, JavaScript, and ActiveX.
- Disable the scripting features in your e-mail programs.
- Regularly back up your critical data.
- Try to make a boot disk if your computer is damaged or compromised.

The following are the details of further discussions on each of these points

Recommendations
- Consult Your System Support Personnel if You Work from Home
  If you are using your broadband access to connect to your employer's network via a VPN or other means, you should take care of the policies or procedures related to the security of the home network. You need to consult the security and support personnel before following any steps written in these documents.

- Use Virus Protection Software
  CERT/CC recommends using antivirus on all Internet-connected computers because the computers connected to the Internet are vulnerable to attacks. There are several antivirus packages available in the market, and they provide regular updates in order to protect your computer from the latest viruses.

- Use a Firewall
  CERT/CC suggests that you need to use a firewall for the product. Intruders are always looking for a vulnerable computer, so there is a chance that they could attack your computer. Network firewalls will provide some degree of protection against these attacks. But it is a fact that firewalls are not enough to protect your computer as you need to have all other measures to completely protect your computer.

- Don't Open Unknown E-mail Attachments
  Unknown e-mails may contain attachments that may harm your computer if they are downloaded. These e-mails are sent for the same purpose, so you should ignore and block the addresses from where you get these e-mails and avoid downloading such e-mails. You might get e-mails from

known sources that may contain viruses. For these e-mails, you need to follow the procedure written below:

- ○ Update your antivirus so that your computer is protected.
- ○ Download the file and save it into the hard disk.
- ○ Scan the file using your antivirus software.
- ○ Open the file.

If you want to have additional protection, you should disconnect the Internet before opening the file. Following the above-mentioned steps is going to help you eliminate the chance of malicious code up to a certain level.

- Don't Run Programs of Unknown Origin
  You should not run programs that are not authorized by a person or a company. You should ensure that you trust the company whose program you are running. You should also not share these programs of unknown origin with your friends as this may contain a Trojan horse.

- Disable Hidden Filename Extensions
  The Windows operating system is quite vulnerable because of the option to "hide file extensions for known file types." You should disable the option so that all the extensions are displayed by Windows. After disabling the option, there will be some file extensions that will remain hidden.

  There is a registry value that, if set, will hide the extensions regardless of user configuration, such as .LNK, which is an extension that will remain hidden even if the user has altered the settings.

- Keep All Applications, Including Your Operating System, Patched
  Vendors are going to release patches of security software whenever they are going to find vulnerabilities. There are several such vendors that provide documentation to get updates and patches. Thus, you should follow the steps

given in the manual to get the updates of the security software.

There are a few applications that are going to check for the updates automatically. There are some vendors that give you the option of automatic updates. If your vendor doesn't provide you the option of automatic updates, then you should periodically check for updates.

- Turn Off Your Computer or Disconnect from the Network When Not in Use
  When you are not using the network, you should disconnect it from the Internet. If your computer is not connected to the Internet, then the intruder will not be able to attack your computer.

- Disable Java, JavaScript, and ActiveX If Possible
  Mobile codes such as Java, JavaScript, and ActiveX also make your computer vulnerable to the attacks. A malicious web developer is going to attach a script to something sent to a website such as a URL, a form, or a database inquiry. When the website responds, the script is transferred to your computer. These attacks can be avoided by disabling the scripting language. Although you will be safe from the attacks, your interaction will be limited. There are many legal sites that use scripts running within the browser to add resourceful features.

- Disable Scripting Features in E-mail Programs
  E-mail programs can also read the scripts, thus making your computer vulnerable to the attacks. As you disable the scripts in your browser, you should also disable this option in your e-mail programs too.

- Make Regular Backups of Critical Data
  You should keep a backup of your data so that if anything happens to your computer, you do not lose the important

data. You should regularly back up your data onto an external storage device, such as a CD or a USB.

- Make a Boot Disk in Case Your Computer is Damaged or Compromised
  To recover from a security breach, hard disk failure, or any other unfortunate event that may result in data loss, you need to create a boot disk on a CD. This is going to help you recover the important data.

Safeguarding Your Data

Why Isn't "More" Better?
There are several software programs that offer additional software along with them. You may even find this software as a free download online. You might be tempted to install this software because you might think that they will prove useful later. You ensure that the source of the software is legitimate, but still, there may be some hidden risks. If others are using your computer, then the risks would increase. These risks become important if you will use your computer to manage your personal finances, store private or sensitive data, and perform work-related confidential activities while you are away from office. The following are some of the steps that are going to help you to protect yourself.

How Can You Protect Your Sensitive Information?

- You should use an updated antivirus software and a firewall. These things are going to protect you from the Trojan horses and many other dangerous viruses that may steal or modify your computer. You should use the updated software and the right settings.
- Scan your computer regularly so that the spyware hidden in software programs may not affect the performance of your computer. Moreover, this is also going to prevent the attacker from accessing your data. The latest antivirus

software have added a feature to detect spyware in your computer.

- Ensure that your software is up-to-date. Edit your antivirus settings to make sure that the updates are installed automatically. If this option is not available, then you should periodically check for the updates.
- Try to evaluate the settings of the software. The default settings of the software may enable all the functionalities that may give a chance to the intruder to hack your computer easily. Thus, you should check the settings of the software that connects you to the Internet and try to apply the highest level of security in order to secure your computer from hacker attacks.
- Avoid using unsaved programs. Do not experiment with your computer by trying out different kinds of software on it. If you have some programs that you do not use, then try uninstalling them from your computer.
- Create separate user accounts for all the users of the computer. This way, others will not be able to see your personal files. Almost all the operating systems give you the option of creating separate user accounts. The operating system also gives you the option of setting the amount of access you want to give to these different accounts. You can even use separate accounts for work and home. This will definitely not protect your computer from the vulnerability of being attacked by an intruder, but it will help to limit the access to the private files.
- Establish guidelines for using the computer. If there is more than one person using the computer, you need to make sure that they follow the necessary guidelines to protect your data.
- You need to use passwords for the private files and encrypt the sensitive information. Passwords and other security features are going to add layers of security to your computer and data. By encrypting the data, you make sure that unauthorized people cannot view data even if they can

physically access it. You can even use full disk encryption because this option is going to help you prevent a thief from even starting your laptop without a passphrase.

- You should follow the rules and regulations provided by the corporation while handling work-related information. These policies will definitely help you protect your device as it will list useful ways to protect your computer. You should be careful with your work-related information, and you should not allow even your family members to access the data.

- Dispose of private and sensitive information in such a way that it is not used in the wrong way. Simply deleting the file will not help because hackers might get access to the files recently deleted. Thus, you need to ensure that you have completely erased the file from the computer.

Real-World Warnings Keep You Safe Online

Why Are These Warnings Important?
Just like the real world, the world of the Internet also presents dangers and benefits. Wrong judgments may be made, equipment might fail, and attackers might target your computer—thus you need to make sure that you take the proper steps to ensure that you protect yourself online. For many kids, the world of the Internet is unfamiliar, so we need to educate them so that they use the Internet the right way.

What Are Some Warnings to Remember?

- Don't trust strangers even if they present you with an attractive offer. The things you find on the Internet are not always true. Anyone can publish information online, so before accepting the offer, you need to ensure that this is a legitimate offer and check if the source is reliable or not. Spoof e-mails are quite common, so before believing in the e-mail, ensure that the e-mail was sent from the right company and it doesn't require any personal information.

- Do not believe in the offers that are sent through e-mails. You might have seen numerous e-mails that promise exceptional rewards. Have you ever wondered why a stranger would want to reward you? There is nothing true in it. They are all spam, hoaxes, or phishing schemes. You should also beware of the pop-up windows as they also contain malicious content.

- Do not let anyone know if you are away from home. When you are not home, your home and personal things are vulnerable to attacks. There are some features that allow you to create an away message when you are away. This is an auto responder, and it is going to reply to all the e-mails that have been sent to you. This is a helpful feature that will let your contacts know that you will not be able to respond right away, but you need to be careful about the wording you use because you do not want the hackers to know that you are not home and they are free to attack your computer. You may say, "I will not have access to e-mail between [dates] and [date]." It is recommended that you also restrict the recipients in your contact list. This will prove useful and save you from attacks. If your e-mail replies to a spam, then the hacker might know that your e-mail is active, and he could attack the computer.

- Make sure valuable and sensitive information is not accessible to everyone. You need to take certain steps to ensure that the information is completely secure. Some of the most basic precautions include locking your computer when you step away. Also using firewalls, antivirus software, and strong passwords may help you protect your data.

- You need to have a backup plan so that your data is backed up regularly. This way, even if you lose your computer or your computer is attacked, you will be able to access your personal documents. Backups also help to identify what has been left and what has been lost.

Tools and Resources

Training Products
Since the introduction of modern technology, training tools have increased and have become a lot more accessible than before. Our learning abilities are the same, but the methods have been transformed from traditional print materials to high-quality videos to self-paced multimedia with multiple paths and multiple representations that allow for multiple methods of learning. If you are interested in training, you need to contact us at info@ arshnet.net or visit our site at http://www.g7security.net to get more information about this training.

FTP Archive
It was established in 1994, and it has the honor of being the first information security repository of its kind. The repository contains certain tools such as software, standards, tools, and other materials that are useful for information security. For more information, please visit http://ftp.cerias.purdue.edu/.

BSD and Linux OS Mirrors
CERIAS offers several open source operating systems as a service. It offers its services to the Purdue community and the security community. Currently, we offer a few open source software such as FreeBSD, OpenBSD, and Ubuntu.

Cassandra Vulnerability Tracking System
This is a tool that allows you to create saved profiles of the applications. The profiles are created by the applications that are currently running on the network. It works with standard configuration hosts. It can also notify you through an e-mail about a new vulnerability. You can view further information at https:// cassandra.cerias.purdue.edu/main/index.html.

NTP Time Server

There are several NTP time servers available under CERIAS. To get further details about them, please visit http://ntp.cerias.purdue.edu.

About the Authors

Anzar Hasan

Anzar Hasan is one of the leading information security audit professionals. He provided his services to Verizon's Internal Audit Department. He is extremely dedicated to implementing the best practices and optimizing the current policies.

Before utilizing his services for Verizon, Anzar worked with the Deloitte & Touche and other notable Fortune 100 companies. He has vast experience in telecommunications/IT/IS ranging from network management to core transport service and wire-line/wireless security. He started off his career in Asia, and he served the Ministry of Communications there. He also got the opportunity to work with a utility company in the Middle East. He worked in the Middle East as a subject matter expert for backbone fiber-optic networks in power grid systems.

Anzar has been a part of numerous turnkey projects of telecom infrastructure in Asia. All these projects were funded by the Asian Development Bank (ADB), International Monetary Fund (IMF), and other United Nations (UN) subsidiaries that were meant for developing countries.

Anzar graduated in electronics from NED University of Engineering and Technology. He is a Certified Information Systems Security Professional (CISSP) and Certified Information Security Manager (CISM). He studied further and took a graduate certificate in business analytics from Southern Methodist University (SMU). He also has graduate certificate in crisis management and business continuity from Massachusetts Institute of Technology (MIT).

Anzar is an avid part of the IEEE study group. He particularly focuses upon the groups that are related to security, reliability, and performance for software defined and virtualized ecosystems (SRPSDVE) and CommSoc rapid standardization team on software-defined networking and network function virtualization (NFV). Anzar is a frequent speaker at international conferences in the telecom industry, such as LTE North America Awards, Small Cells North America Network, Virtualization North America, and many more. Anzar also got the chance to serve on the board of the American Cyber Security Association. This is an independent, nonprofit, global association. He currently resides in Dallas, Texas, with his wife and two boys.

Abbas Mirza

Abbas Mirza is one of the renowned personalities in the computer world. He has over fifteen years of experience in architecture, analysis, design, development, implementation, and management of information technology systems. He is the laureate of the Computerworld Honors Program 2013.

He is currently a part of PepsiCo, and he is showing some amazing leadership skills as a BI data management specialist. He has shown the capacity to build and enable cross-functional teams to execute highly productive projects. Abbas has expertise in complex development projects in the environment of highly sensitive and secure IT solutions at large global corporations such as Nortel, AT&T, and other notable Fortune 100 companies.

In the year 2010, Abbas was able to launch the G7 Security app under the Arshnet Technologies. This app is currently available on App Store. It is one of the most effective initiatives that will help to spread awareness, and it will help to develop defense against cyber attacks.

G7 Security is a cybersecurity research and global information security services entity. This particular entity was developed by Abbas and Anzar so that they could make a head start on the initiative of cybersecurity.

This entity offers research and development, information sharing, and collaboration. In addition to this, it offers various services for the information and cybersecurity community. The efforts made to develop the G7 Security app were recognized in Computerworld's Mobile Access awards category for the innovative application of IT. The major aim of this app was to extend the distribution of digital information, programs, and services through mobile devices. This was the reason due to which it was able to reach into the areas where the use of mobile devices is quite common. The Computerworld Honors Program honors those who try to develop visionary applications of information technology through which they try promote positive social, economic, and educational change.

Abbas is honored with the title of being the founder of iSecurity and Agile groups on LinkedIn. These products have over fifty thousand members all over the world. Abbas also works as an advisor to young start-ups. He guides them in the areas of application development and data security principles.

Abbas earned his bachelor's degree in business computer information systems from Midwestern State University, and he was able to get his advanced technical training from Southern Methodist University (SMU).

Index